Salem Academy and College
FRIENDS of the LIBRARY

Gift of

The Friends of
the Library

# Binding Cultures

# BLACKS IN THE DIASPORA

Darlene Clark Hine, John McCluskey, Jr., and David Barry Gaspar

*General Editors*

# Binding Cultures

## Black Women Writers in Africa and the Diaspora

■

Gay Wilentz

Indiana University Press
Bloomington & Indianapolis

Manufactured in the United States of America

Library of Congress Cataloging-in-Publication Data

Wilentz, Gay Alden, date.
Binding cultures : Black Women Writers in Africa and the Diaspora/Gay Wilentz.
  p. cm. — (Blacks in the diaspora)
Includes bibliographical references and index.
ISBN 0-253-36585-6. — ISBN 0-253-20714-2 (pbk.)
1. American literature—Afro-American authors—History and criticism. 2. West African literature (English)—Women authors—History and criticism. 3. Literature, Comparative—West African (English) and American. 4. Literature, Comparative—American and West African (English) 5. American literature—Women authors—History and criticism. 6. Women and literature—United States. 7. Women and literature—Africa, West. 8. Afro-American women in literature. 9. Women, Black, in literature. 10. Folklore in literature. I. Title. II. Series.
PS153.N5W48 1992
810.9'9287'08996—dc20                                        91-27069

2 3 4 5 96 95 94 93

*To*
*all*
*those*
*born*
*in the*
*diaspora*
*and to*
*my*
*ancestors*

If you surrendered to the air,
you could ride it.

TONI MORRISON

# Contents

■

# ACKNOWLEDGMENTS

Certainly no work of this sort, spanning continents and cultures, could possibly have been done alone. More people than I can name here have helped me with this work—from growing up in New York City to teaching literacy in Anson County, North Carolina, and learning about life in West Africa—but I acknowledge just a few of the many individuals and families for the awareness and understanding they have given me to help complete this study.

I would like to thank all those at the University of Texas who helped with the inception of this book and directed my approach and production: Bernth Lindfors, Jane Marcus, and Ramón Saldívar for their vision, time, and patience; Beverly Stoeltje, John Lamphear, Keith Byerman, and Michael King for their expertise and friendship. Others in Texas who added to my understanding: Kofi Anyidoho, Elliott Banks, Marlies Gättens, Alma Haertlein, Rolando Hinajosa, Tayoba Ngenge, Emmanuel Prophete, Micheline Rice-Maximin, Melvin Wade, Arnie Williams, George Wright, and most importantly, Wilson Harris and James Sledd.

I am grateful to the Fulbright program for supporting my research and trip to Nigeria. Deep thanks goes to Flora Nwapa, who took me under her wing, and to Donatus Nwoga, who helped facilitate my stay and formulate my thoughts. Others in Nigeria I would like to thank are: Chinua Achebe, Ernest Emenyonu, Lillian Jenkins, Ada Mere, Charles Nnolin, Chimalum Nwankwo, Femi Ojo-Ade, Kamene Okonjo, Chidi Okonkwo, Juliet Okonkwo, Beatrice and Francis Sefe, 'Zulu Ṣofọla, Theo Vincent, and the Ukwuese family. I would like to thank East Carolina University for the two research grants I received to give me the time to finish this book. Deep thanks also goes to Paule Marshall, who took the time to talk to me about the "Ibos" who walked. Further thanks goes to colleagues and friends at other universities who presented ideas and gave support along the way: Alex Albright, Abena Busia, Rhonda Cobham-Sanders, Louise de Salvo, Marie Farr, Sally Ann Fergusen, Sandy Govan, Abdul Jan-Mohammed, Norman Rosenfeld, and Keats Sparrow. To Karla Holloway and Joyce Pettis, thanks is not enough for their constant encouragement, friendship, and support. Without my research assistants, I couldn't have made this as complete a study as it is: Joseph Cambell, Carolyn Sutton, Cindy Thompson-Rumple, Christine Russell, and Traci Treat.

I would also like to thank Iris Tillman Hill for her first reading, and Sandy Eisdorfer for her amazing energy and constant support. Special thanks goes to those people who are always there for me: Michael Bassman, Carol Castellano, Daniel Dawson, Julie Fay, John Inniss, Ana Sisnett, and especially, Sandy Shattuck. This study could not have been finished without these three friends who kept me on track: the expert editing by and deep discussions with Kathy Whaley, the emotional support and copyediting skills of Gloria Chance, and the editing, research skills, vision, and advocacy of Kathleen Cusick.

Finally, my deepest gratitude goes to the memory of my grandparents, Mack, Pearl, David, and Lena; my parents, Warren and Stefani; my parents-in-law, Edward and Doris; my brothers Wayne and Michael; my uncles, aunts, and cousins, especially Jim, Amy, Robert, Connie, and Kermit; my whole extended family; and of course, my husband and traveling partner, John Sabella, whose support has made this work possible.

# INTRODUCTION

Perhaps in more than Phillis Wheatley's
biological life is her mother's signature
made clear.

Alice Walker

## I.

The history of Black women's literature started long before Black women were finally allowed their right to literacy. Their
literature and other creative art were oral, rooted in storytelling
and the African/African-American folk tradition. "Because Black
women rarely gained access to literary expression, Black women-
identified bonding and folk culture have often gone unrecorded
except through our individual lives and memories" (Bethel 179).
Thus, when Black women began to write creative works, they
looked back to their foremothers to recreate these stories. This is
true for both African and African-American women, but since the
line between the Americans and their African past was forcibly
broken by their dispersion into the Americas, they have had to
make a larger imaginative leap than their African sisters. Harlem
Renaissance writer Zora Neale Hurston, the spiritual and literary
foremother of many modern African-American women writers,
drew from the orature of her African culture turned slave culture in
her tales, novels, and short stories. Contemporary African-
American women writers have had to take their search one step
further to envision their African foremothers, and now sisters,
whose use of oral traditions and storytelling to impart cultural
values has been passed down from generation to generation. From

Hurston's "If I never see you no' mo' on earth, Ah'll meet you in Africa" (*Their Eyes* 231) to Alice Walker's Afro-utopian community in the rural South; from Toni Morrison's Solomon who deserts his family to join the "Flying Africans" to Paule Marshall's Igbos who take one look at the New World and decide to walk on home; in these and other examples, we see Black American women focusing on Africa not only as historical ancestor, political ally, and basis for ideological stance but as part of a continuum in which Black women, before the slave trade and since, have recorded cultural history and values through their stories.

My study explores the cultural bonds between African and African-American women as illustrated in the writings of six contemporary authors in West Africa and the United States. The major texts under discussion are four novels and two plays, originally written in English, as well as references to the authors' other works. The study focuses on the concept of "generational continuity"—the passing on of cultural values and personal history—as traditionally a woman's domain.[1] Anthropologist Nancy Tanner defines this societal structure as "matrifocal": "A kinship system with a matrifocal emphasis is one in which *the role of the mother is central in terms of cultural values* . . . and affective ties" (152; emphasis added). I examine this matrifocal system of education in relation to the contemporary African woman writer as well as to the cultural continuity of African values and customs in the New World. Moreover, the portrayal of the society and cultural life that the African women present is used as a criterion for the exploration of Black American women writers' creation of an African model for a more integrated African-American society.

Writing on Black women writers within the context of a white, male, Eurocentric literary canon, I have had to develop an alternative critical methodology to offset many ethnocentric, preconceived notions and prejudices regarding what actually constitutes creative art. As a critic of African/African-American and ethnic women's literature, I find it imperative to use a literary criticism which is neither racist, patriarchal, nor Eurocentric.[2] The difficulty arises in finding a comprehensive criticism not grounded in white male Western Christian hegemony. The acceptance of the literature of white women has been marginal enough; African and African-American literatures, even when written by men, have received little attention in mainstream literary circles. All writings from the Third World and minority groups in North America have been appraised by the biased criticism of the literary establishment in the United States and Britain. Literatures of diaspora cultures are evaluated, for the most part, by the confines of manmade boundaries such as "national" or "continental" studies. So, until recently, the writing of Black women of the African diaspora, having neither gender nor color in its favor, has suffered the greatest neglect; moreover, canonical hegemony and lack of critical attention have led to a distorted view of the work when acknowledged.

In response to this hegemony, committed critics of oppressed peoples' literature agree that we cannot separate the literature from the historical or cultural context in which it was written. Although Frederic Jameson does not apply his statement to the work of writers from oppressed groups, in his essay "Towards Dialectical Criticism," he states another objective of cultural criticism—that the job of the critic is to expose the work of art from under the layers of censorship and prejudice of the dominant culture: "The process of criticism is not so much an interpretation of content as it is a revealing of it, a laying bare, a restoration of the original message, the original experience beneath the distortions of the various kinds of censorship that have been at work upon it" (404). "Laying bare" the work of an "excluded" writer, as Lillian Robinson puts it, includes a reevaluation not only of the oppressed culture but of the critic's own assumptions—no matter what the critic's background.[3] Moreover, the task of exploring works of cultures suppressed by the dominant culture needs an interdisciplinary approach to criticism, an examination of the literature's historicity and social significance, attention to its oral/folkloric inheritance, and an understanding of the writer's commitment to reflect and often reform the culture that the literature represents.

Especially germane to this study is a Black Feminist criticism primarily concerned with defining cultural imperatives unique to the experience of the Black woman throughout the diaspora. Concurrently, there is an ongoing, consolidated movement by those involved with scholarly research on Black women to formulate a broad-based critical approach.[4] In the last fifteen years, Black Feminist scholarship has developed rapidly as a moving force in critical theory. Black women and other feminist scholars have explored the dimensions of generational and cultural continuity for people of African descent, particularly regarding women; in many areas, these scholars have broken through the often narrow, Eurocentric, and almost exclusively male focus of traditional scholarship. Furthermore, there has been a flowering of studies, exploring Black women's literature through historical, cultural, feminist, and lesbian perspectives, using both traditional and Marxist methodologies. In "Towards a Black Feminist Criticism," a germinal work often cited by critics, Barbara Smith presents an overview:

> The breadth of [the critic's] familiarity with [Black women] writers would have shown her that not only is theirs a verifiable historical tradition that parallels in time the tradition of Black men and white women writing in this country, but that thematically, stylistically, aesthetically, and conceptually Black women writers manifest common approaches towards the act of creating literature as a direct result of the specific political, social, and economic experience they have been obliged to share. . . . The Black feminist critic would find innumerable commonalities in works by Black women . . . [and] would be constantly aware of the political implications of her work and would assert the connections between it and the political situation of all Black women. (163–64)

My own methodology is primarily cultural: a composite of Marxist, feminist, and Afrocentric criticism, utilizing an interdisciplinary approach consisting of historical, sociological, anthropological, and folkloric material. Although I compare the writers' thematic concerns, stylistic designs, and ideological stances, the major thrust of this study is to explore how cultural traditions have been passed down from African mother to slave mother to African-American mother to teach the "patient craft" of their cultural heritage to continuing generations of women and men (Marcus 85). For African and African-American women writers, generational and cultural continuity—"to look back through our mothers"—is seen as a woman's domain. Orature and, consequently, literature are part of many women's daily struggle to communicate, converse, and pass on values to their own and other children, and one another. In defining the connection between art and work, socialist feminist critic Jane Marcus links the written creations with the oral tradition of women storytellers and singers of songs:

> History is preserved not in the art object but in the tradition of *making* the art object. . . . It is eaten, it is worn; culture consists in passing on the technique of its making. Stories are made to be told, and songs to be sung. In the singing and the telling, they are changed. . . . Transformation, rather than permanence, is at the heart of this aesthetic, as it is at the heart of most women's lives. (85)

Accordingly, I have found it most useful to understand the oral voicings that have preceded the written works, for these voicings are part of a cultural preparedness in the writers that exposes generational and cultural continuity in the works themselves.[5]

Furthermore, I have looked at the writings, both African and African-American, as "diaspora" literature which transcends national boundaries and reflects a cultural lineage beyond even that of familial ancestry. Until recently, there was little focus on women's role in the creation of a diaspora culture and on the commonalities that exist in female modes of cultural production throughout the African diaspora. The concept of "diaspora literature" as women's literature calls into question imposed, manmade literary boundaries such as "Nigerian," "American," or even "African" literature in relation to the writings of Black women; a diaspora perspective opens up relationships and connections not easily addressed even in continental studies. Without this broader exploration of the works by women of African descent on both sides of the Atlantic, many of the signs and meanings of the discourse are lost. Finally, my personal experience as a woman and a member of a diaspora culture informs this work.

This book consists of two sections: "The Africans" and "The African-Americans." Throughout, I explore the concept of generational and cultural continuity within a traditional African context. I take a dialectic approach in terms of how the female characters pass on their cultural values and traditions and how the authors themselves, as women, communicate their cultural heritage to generations of readers. The first section of the study is germinal because the traditional values of the writers' society are utilized as criteria for an examination of the cultural values and heritage in the African-American section. The African section includes a chapter each on Nigerian writer Flora Nwapa and Ghanaians Efua Sutherland and Ama Ata Aidoo. The discussion centers on how the cultural mores and value systems are passed down through the female members of the society, especially through and to the children. I also explore the use of orature as a method of education and the orality of the writing style of each author.

The second section, "The African-Americans," contains a chapter each on three contemporary Black women writers—Alice Walker, Toni Morrison, and Paule Marshall—who portray their African heritage as an alternative to mainstream America. Through the cultural retentions that have survived since slavery, these women are attempting to reflect, (re)discover, and (re)articulate their African roots; their aim is to help build communities more in line with African cultural values. As women, they take on their traditional role as educators of present and future generations to voice their heritage, which has been distorted and effaced for many in the Black community through imposed dominant cultural values and attempts at assimilation. Pertinent to their aims is a use of the orature in their writings as a method of uncovering and recovering their collective past.

As this study of women's literature in Africa and the diaspora invites multifaceted comparisons, I necessarily have had to set boundaries to contain the research. My first limitations were linguistical and geographical: I have chosen to focus on those works originally written in English and, in the first section, on writers from West Africa since this area was the major target of the transatlantic slave trade.[6] Much research has been done in reconstituting the history of the Africans as they were forcibly brought from West Africa to the United States; Alex Haley's *Roots*, set in the Gambia, has received the most attention. Yet cultural traces such as the Yoruba churches in Harlem, Igbo, Akan, and Mende names in the southern coastal areas, and food preferences and folklore throughout the Southeast attest to the areas from whence the slaves came: Senegal, Ghana, Nigeria, Liberia, Ivory Coast, Angola, as well as the smaller coastal states of West Africa such as Sierra Leone and the Gambia.

My second limitation was that of genre. I have focused on two forms—the novel and the play—with supplemental references to the short story. Many have argued that these forms are the most approachable in terms of reconstructing social values and as vehicles for social change; moreover, the world represented in these forms often reflects (although dialectically) the culture in more direct ways than in a form such as poetry. In an African context, drama as performed art is oral in nature and emphasizes the relationship between the playwright and the audience. According to Kofi Awoonor, drama is an indigenous art form (69-72). The short story has been seen by African writers and critics alike as an expansion of the African folk tale, and it clearly retains its oral antecedents. Although it is harder to make that kind of statement concerning the novel, a European genre, African critics such as Chinweizu, Jemie, and Maduibuike have suggested that the modern African novel has evolved from the African epic in terms of structure, content, and the world it creates. Moreover, Russian theorist M. M. Bakhtin has also argued that even the traditional European novel incorporates oral antecedents ("Epic and Novel" 3–40). For much of the literature of Africa and the diaspora, the debt to the orature is so evident that I have neologized the two disparate terms to convey the process: "oraliterature." Oraliterature refers to written creative works which retain elements of the orature that informed them. In particular, the works I have chosen reflect the authors' aims to encapsulate the orality of the spoken word and the active presentation of the oral tradition within the confines of fiction.[7]

A third limitation relates to intercultural influences. Although many aspects of African-American culture have permeated African society in recent times, this study is confined to the influences of African culture on Black America. Since Africa is the original source of the values, customs, and traditions that have crossed and recrossed the Atlantic, my direction is from Africa outward into the diaspora, in this case into the United States.

One final concern needs to be addressed at this point. Despite my emphasis on the validity of African cultural influences on Black America, there are, naturally, dissimilarities in the way African women writers approach their own society and the way African-American women perceive their adaptation of African culture—life in Africa as distinct from "African lifestyles." The African women see their culture and traditions in both a positive and a negative light—as a life-giving force as well as a restriction of women's rights. For the African-American writer, Africa, as a symbol of an alternative practice to mainstream American life, evolved into Afro-America after the last slaves were forcibly brought into the United States. Although there is a strong sense of cultural continuity between Africa and the Americas, this diaspora perspective does not always preclude understanding or acceptance of the ancestors' homeland. A good example of this dichotomy is illustrated by Alice Walker's *The Color Purple*. In this novel, which I discuss in detail in chapter 4, Walker's portrayal of a West African country can be unfairly biased at times, exposing merely the restrictive codes and cruelty of the society at the expense of the more humane aspects of the culture; yet her utopian community at the end of the novel is a Southern rural recreation of an African village. Furthermore, she espouses these communal values as a goal for African-American communities to aim toward.

Finally, I would like to make some introductory remarks about the identification of African values examined in this study as well as the concept of "generational continuity." Modern scholars of African literature, history, and philosophy have examined the cultural mores and values systems of precolonial Africa, distinguishing African societal norms from Western values and mores. Although the differences have been overstressed at times, there are definitely variants in how human existence is culturally evoked. Probably the most thoroughly investigated disparity concerns the individual's responsibility to the community. Western culture, particularly in the twentieth century, has had a strongly capitalistic, individualistic approach to community structures: What is good for me will be good for the community. Thus, the heavy emphasis on the acquisition of material wealth. Historically, and even today in many African societies, there has been greater emphasis on the individual's accountability to the group. As Nigerian playwright 'Zulu Şofọla, commented to me: "One can object [follow one's individual notions] but not so far as to destroy the fiber of the society." Another major disparity involves family structure. Many anthropological studies have looked at the nuclear versus the extended family—European/African, White/Black; in contrast to the nuclear family, the extended family is a way of branching out to a whole community through marriage. In this system, your responsibility is to all the children of the community, not merely your own. Coupled with consciousness of a continuum from the ancestors to the present generation and their descendants, this system creates a world view which, in many ways, conflicts with Western notions of family and society.

Concurrently, another dialectic is at work: Within an African community, even after European intervention, men and women have had strictly defined roles in both public and private life, whereas in Western countries the society emphasizes mainly the male role in public life and the female role in private life. Notwithstanding some earlier Western scholarship on African societies which defined a dual sex role system as antithetical to women's rights, this kind of societal organization produced a more independent woman than did the male-dominated system in the West. For example, in precolonial West Africa, women had their own native courts and were often in charge of the domestic affairs of all the villagers, both male and female. In Western countries, there is only one legal system, presumably for all the citizens of a community, but that system is totally male-oriented. I mention this aspect of African culture cursorily at this point to lead into a finer definition of "generational continuity" and to show how this process of oral transmission of cultural values and education comes under women's domain in a dual sex role system.

In the introduction to *Women Writers of Black Africa*, Lloyd Brown clearly states his understanding of the cultural imperatives of men and women in African society:

> I must emphasize at this point that I am not attributing to these writers some *inherent* and universally female point of view. . . ; what I am suggesting is that in writing about women and their men, these writers emphasize that the experience, identity, and role of a woman are all distinguishable from a man's, in *culturally definable terms.* . . . (21; emphasis added)

With regard to the oral transmission of customs and values from one generation to the next, it is women who most often fulfill the role of tale teller and instructor. Igbo sociologist Ada Mere comments on this aspect of women's role in the society: "[Women] are the most primary and constant agents of child socialization" (3); furthermore, women, as agents of this education, "are the mainstay of oral tradition" (15). Even a problematic study such as Oladele Taiwo's *Female Novelists of Modern Africa* corroborates Mere's point:[8]

> The folk tale is used in a more dramatic manner to initiate children and adolescents into their cultural heritage. . . . The leader of the performance may be a man or a woman. But it is often the woman

who plays the part because she is not as tired after the day's work as the man. The content of the tale is moralistic and the purpose of the presentation is didactic. (8)

I would suggest that rather than attributing women's primary role in cultural education to the fact that they have a less strenuous day than their male counterparts, Taiwo might have commented on the nature of women's defined role in family and community socialization. Taiwo himself admits to this later in his book, referring to women's historical domain in "formulating and codifying these modes of expression in traditional society" (219).

Generational continuity is not specifically African, since women from all traditional societies (and some modern ones) have produced unwritten volumes for their children and children's children; still, there are identifiable values and traditions which flow throughout the African diaspora: "Just as the biological and social ties of mothers to their children continue in altered forms after the umbilicus has been cut and the child has been weaned, so precolonial ideas about women span the spaces between past and present, Africa and the New World, to reappear in striking ways" (Rushing 166). Not only have ideas from and about African women before colonialism continued through generations and across oceans, but the way in which women have passed on their cultural heritage has endured. It is most probable that by telling the history of one's people to future generations and imparting cultural values to the children of those generations, Black women throughout the diaspora have kept their heritage alive.

## II.

The theoretical framework of this study hinges on the relationship between women and the oral tradition, particularly in regard to Black women's historicity and women's role in orally transmitting the values and mores of their culture. While much writing on Black women has already uncovered the commonalities among women of the diaspora, formerly hidden by hegemonic western cultural/literary practice, the major intent of my study is to analyze *how* these cultural connections have been passed on within Africa and the diaspora through the writings of representative women:

what is the process of cultural preparation, as Robert Farris Thompson calls it, that women throughout the diaspora have employed to tell the tale of their heritage? Bernice Johnson Reagon calls this process "mothering" and states: "One can use the concept of a mothering generation to mean the way the entire community organizes itself to nurture itself and its future generations" ("African Diaspora Women" 177). On familial, community, and diasporal levels, this process is inscribed in the orature of the culture, the stories of the women. Therefore, a preliminary investigation of the "mothering" process of generational and cultural continuity, as well as female genres of oral art forms may be of use. To do this, I examine the importance of the oral tradition and orature in African society and woman's role in passing on the values of her culture, and I cite the (limited) existing scholarship on women's province in the oral tradition. In addition, my own experiences living with three generations of women in Eastern Nigeria and spending two years in Sierra Leone inform this discussion.

Because of the nature of and prejudices in the research to date, there is not nearly enough material specifically on women's function in the folk culture. Colonialist, patriarchal scholarship disregards, for the most part, the manner in which African women utilize oral art forms. In the introduction to *Women and Folklore* (1975), Claire Farrer emphatically states that although there has been "lipservice paid to the importance of women's expressive behavior," it is clear that "when a collector had a choice between a story as told by a man or as told by a woman, the man's version was chosen." Even when women informants are mentioned, the manner and style in which they produce and pass on their tales have been largely ignored. Farrer goes on to say that women "may have known and bequeathed a rich traditional heritage, but information is sketchy concerning the extent of [their] folklore repertoire" (xix). Since Farrer's collection, more work has been done in this area, but still the lack of data and interest has distorted women's traditional position, especially within dual sex role, African societal organization, which stresses strictly defined roles for both men and women. Therefore, it follows that the type of stories and perhaps even the manner of production might have gender-specific qualities.[9] Western or Western-trained (male) scholars, who have done most of the research on the oral tradition, often disregard the manner in which African women create and pass on orature. Although recent studies give voice to an Afrocentric, woman-centered discourse, this male, Western bias not only has hindered the exploration of the orature in African communities but also has affected critical attitudes toward and understanding of the writings of women—since the orature informs the language and structure of the works (Davies and Graves, *Ngambika* 17). It is the dialectical relationship between the orature that women create and the oraliterature of the writers in this study that I address here.

According to Jan Vansina, "oral tradition" encompasses both oral history and orature. Oral history "deals with accounts of events" while the orature is an artistic "interpretation of experience," even though both aspects of the oral tradition may come from the same sources (13). Under the rubric of orature are found the folk tales, songs, and proverbs examined in this study. These and other forms of orature, Vansina revealingly suggests, are "among the main well springs of what we call 'culture.' . . . Such cultural contents are transmitted to children in the process of learning the language and learning how to behave" (7; 124). In discussing this significant aspect of the orature, Vansina does not expound on the gender of the storyteller, but there is (hidden) evidence to lead us to suspect that these undocumented storytellers were women. As I argue in more detail later, implicit in the role of women as mothers, aunts, and grandmothers is the transmission of existing messages of culture to the children.

Examining the relationship between the orature and contemporary African literature is of paramount concern to many of its writers, male and female. Encoded in the writings are histories of oral art which helped shape societies and which remains despite so-called modernization. Although West African communities today are no longer primarily oral cultures, much of this way of life is present within the literate population and certainly within literary creations. What has survived is, in linguist Walter Ong's terms, a "participation in a kind of corporate retrospection" as well as a society which "regards highly those wise old men and women who specialize in conserving [the culture], who know and can tell the stories of the days of old" (40). Ong brings up two points relevant to this study—the collective nature of oral cultures and the respect generated by the wisdom of the elders, including venerable women. Ong further expounds on the relationship between an oral and a collective culture which is illustrated in the works of the women writers discussed in this section: "Because of its physical constitution as sound, the spoken word proceeds from the human interior and manifests human beings to one another as conscious interiors, as persons, the spoken word forms human beings into close knit groups" (74). Of course, there is an apparent contradiction inherent in applying the conditions of orature to a written work, but it seems to me that this fusion is exactly what these authors are doing. The process is further clarified in light of Achebe's understanding of Igbo, and presumably West African, cosmological sense of oppositions—"Wherever something stands, something else will stand beside it"—since the written literature can no longer be oral yet it encapsulates the orality of its culture, creating oraliterature.[10]

As Ong points out, a traditional world view is based on assumptions of a collective nature, that there is a body of expressive knowledge that each community is aware of and, to some extent, abides by. These values are encapsulated in the oral traditions of the culture, and women play a large part by communicating this body of knowledge to their children, as Vansina notes above. In *Culture, Tradition and Society in the West African Novel*, Emmanuel Obiechina emphasizes the significance of the collective nature of these oral traditions in modern African life. In evoking African culture within the context of their writings, the authors derive meaning from a collective world view based on traditional practices: "The traditional individual's apprehension of reality is therefore the collectively shared vision of reality certified by custom" (40). He explains further that "the most noticeable difference between novels written by native West Africans and those by non-natives using West African settings is the important position which the representation of oral tradition is given by the first, and its almost complete absence in the second" (25). Although Obiechina fails to examine any women writers—even his fellow Nigerian, Flora Nwapa—in his study, the absence of these writers from studies like Obiechina's does not indicate the absence of orature in their works.

Specifically, these women writers are concerned with women's role as "custodians of the traditions," a major theme of this study. As Filomina Chioma Steady contends in *The Black Woman Cross-Culturally*: "The woman . . . represents the ultimate value in [African] life, namely the continuation of the group" (32). And her service in continuing the group is intellectual/spiritual as well as physical. In these matrifocal societies, women's place in the community is assessed in terms of "cultural elaboration and valuation as well as the structural centrality of mother roles. . . ." (Tanner 154). In examining a "mothering process" of cultural transmission, it is essential also to remember that the term "mother" includes not merely the biological mother but co-mothers, grandmothers, aunts, older sisters, community women. The elaborate structure of a family compound in West Africa attests to both the predominance of women's position in family and community life and the emphasis on the young women following the traditions in the same manner as their mothers and grandmothers.

Historically and today, a woman's function in the compound extends to the entire village communal life, but there have been changes which have limited women's role as citizen in her own right. The balanced interrelationship between the woman and her community was disrupted during colonialism, and that disruption has added to women's present-day second-class citizenship. In "Female Employment and Family Organization in West Africa," Niara Sudarkasa examines a precolonial system which, although male-dominated, incorporated women's power:

> In traditional West Africa the compound was usually the unit of political organization, and decisions within the compound had implications for the wider political units whether this was a village or a town. Thus wives, mothers, sisters, or daughters could exert direct political influence over males, or they themselves could play important roles by virtue of their position of authority, power or influence in their natal or affinal compounds. (53)

For the African authors examined here, the dialectical relationship of women to their community is framed by the position of women in precolonial Africa and the changes made by colonialism and neo-colonialism. But throughout history, the role of women and the collective nature of women's work have informed the life of the community even as they have been devalued by the scholarship of men.

The collectivity of women's work is becoming more fully documented through studies like those cited here, but it may be precisely because of women's artistic collectivity that their contribution to the oral tradition has not been widely acknowledged. It is easier for researchers to investigate a few "master" storytellers than to look at the many women who, on any day, are passing on the values of their culture through oral art forms. Still, a number of researchers, critics, and writers have investigated this aspect of oral culture. A. C. Jordan, in researching his own culture, sought out old women who were renowned as storytellers to record them in his *Tales from Southern Africa*. Other anthropologists and oral historians have used women informants as well, although these researchers are not in the majority. Jordan indicates the importance of the compound: "The homestead is probably the smallest unit in which such performances occurred. Within the homestead the older women, usually the grandmothers or old aunts, were the storytellers" (xv). Mineke Schipper's *Unheard Words* documents the relationship of women to the oral tradition in most of the so-called Third World; moreover this extensive study reinforces Jordan's comments about older women being considered the best storytellers, challenging the notion that men were the only "master" storytellers (13). Lloyd Brown, who also quotes from Jordan (revealing the need for much more work to be done in this area), prefaces his book on African women writers by referring to their historicity as oral artists: "The contributions of women to African literature have not been limited to the modern period. Women have always played a considerable role, as storytellers and performers, in the oral tradition" (14). Studies such as Beverly Mack's "Songs from Silence: Hausa Women's Poetry" reflect exciting new directions and concrete examples of the relationship of orature to literature for women artists.

Most importantly, the African women writers themselves testify to the influence of their foremothers' orature on their works. Abena Busia, poet and critic, sees Black women's "herstories" as collective self-definition, a chief strategy being "the incorporation of the folk culture, oral tradition in particular, into written texts" (3). Furthermore, in interviews in both Schipper's and Taiwo's books, many of the writers speak of learning their craft from their mothers, grandmothers, or older women in the community. For example, Nigerian writer Buchi Emecheta remarks that she learned storytelling skills from her grandmother and other community women "in moonlight sessions when she was young" (Taiwo 100). Especially pertinent to this study, all of the African women writers discussed refer to both the power encoded in their foremothers' stories and their responsibility to pass on these stories to future generations. During one of our conversations, Flora Nwapa explicitly acknowledged her debt to the women's folk stories she heard when she was young; in addition, the embryonic ideas for *Efuru* and *Idu* came from her mother. Both Efua Sutherland and Ama Ata Aidoo are profoundly aware of the legacy of the orature which they received from their mothers and stress women's role in passing on oral traditions; moreover, Aidoo states that the legend on which her play *Anowa* is based was one she heard from her mother. The understanding that these writers' craft is something handed down to them from their foremothers underscores their commitment to pass on this cultural knowledge to their children. Efua Sutherland has stated that the most important work an African writer can do is "to write for the children" (Lautré 193).

## III.

In the early stages of writing this book, I had an intriguing conversation with Donatus Nwoga, then head of the University of Nigeria's Institute for African Studies. In discussing the transmission of values and traditions from African mother to African-American mother, Nwoga raised the question of purpose: Why examine these generational and cultural connections? What will this knowledge mean to those "children" of the diaspora? Having grown up in a diaspora culture, I had an intuitive feeling that this knowledge was *power*, and the (re)vision the authors present back up those "unscientific" feelings. Moreover, the thrust in Black literary theory and history since the early 1980s has reinforced this view. But it was reading Bernice Johnson Reagon's "African Diaspora Women: The Making of Cultural Workers" which clarified for me the richness in comprehending these diasporal connections. In her own work, Reagon speaks of realizing that these connections extend beyond content:

> I began to think that maybe the culture offered more than data content; that maybe the culture offered a process, a way to get things done, a way to collect, assemble, and present material; *that maybe the culture offered a methodology for these activities, a theory for use.* . . . (167)

The methodology that Reagon describes is that of the mothering process. As I noted earlier, this process is a way of preserving (and dialectically, sometimes challenging) cultural and generational continuity. Who were the undocumented cultural workers who prepared the new soil to adapt the traditions? It can be argued that part of the cultural achievement of Africans in the Americas has come from the diaspora women who "mothered" African-American culture into being.[11] To foreground my analysis of the writers in the African-American section, I examine Reagon's process of mothering in relation to Raymond Williams's theory of "residual" and "emergent" culture, specifically in regard to some critics' objections to the supposed polarities of Afrocentric/ Eurocentric dichotomies. Through this discussion and the study as a whole, I hope to elucidate other ways of knowing—women's ways.[12]

In "Beyond Essentialism: Rethinking Afro-American Cultural Theory," Elliott Butler-Evans claims that most interpretations of African-American texts are overdetermined by "ideological agendas" (123) and reinforce binary oppositions such as Afrocentric/ Eurocentric (125). Although there is much to agree with in this thought-provoking essay, Butler-Evans falls into his own trap. He sets up his own opposition between essentialist texts which valorize the group, focusing on the "unified black subject" (129), and those works out of the reach of essentialist critics which problematize African-American experience. One problem I see with this approach is that many of the writings by African-American women—including Toni Cade Bambara, whom he cites—both problematize the culture *and* are Afrocentric. The whole notion of Afrocentricity inscribed in women's writings poses its own dialectics. An Afrocentric sense of "otherness" within self and culture, described by Achebe, presents a resistance to the fixed positions encoded in the concept itself. Moreover, as women in an African-based society, these writers are constantly working out their role as Other to the hegemony of Eurocentric culture and Other to their men.

To further elucidate the dialectics of Afrocentric discourse, I turn to Williams's discussion of "residual" and "emergent" culture in *Problems in Materialism and Culture*. Although Williams does not examine his theory in relation to a multicultural society, one can easily appropriate it. According to Williams, "residual" culture reaches "back to those meanings and values which were created in real societies in the past" and "represents areas of human experience ... which the dominant culture undervalues or opposes, or cannot even recognize" (386). African-based cultural traditions can be seen as a residual culture denied/ignored by the dominant group. "Emergent" culture, on the other hand, is defined by "new meanings and values, new practices, new significances and experiences [which] are constantly being created" (385). In this case, the civil rights movement or other cultural movements in the 1960s might be considered emergent. But Williams hastens to remind us that these are dialectical relationships so that residual/emergent cultures may over(or inter)lap each other and the dominant culture as well—which often incorporates or "coopts" these cultural practices. For example, the Black Aesthetic and cultural nationalist movement in the 1960s represents an interworking of residual and emergent culture, which was at once both oppositional to the dominant culture *and* incorporated by it. Although the Black Panthers and other nationalist groups were seen as a threat to the dominant order, the slogan "Black is Beautiful"—based on an idealized African physique—was quickly coopted by a line of cosmetics.

In examining the dialectics of residual and emergent cultural practices, Williams also includes another distinction in counter-hegemonic movements implied above: "oppositional" and "alternative" (385). When a practice becomes oppositional, the dominant culture must incorporate it, or it becomes subject to attack. "Alternative" practice is different. It is often tolerated by the dominant culture because of its isolation from and nonthreatening relationship to dominant cultural practices (there is, however, a fine line between the two, Williams notes, since alternative can easily become oppositional). While oppositional supposes a desire to change existing order, alternative theoretically signifies a disregard of existing order. Much of African-American (male) literature has been oppositional, since the focus of the works tends to be an articulation of self as opposed to white men/white society. But the women may tell another story. Like their spiritual foremother Hurston, the African-American writers discussed here demonstrate that documenting alternative cultural practices may open up other ways of seeing which have been lost both in opposition to and incorporation by the dominant culture. One might say that the writings themselves are part of an alternative cultural practice, challenging the "canon" of African-American literature and criticism—and the practice is both residual and emergent. This alternative practice does not pose Afrocentric against Eurocentric as binary oppositions; rather, it exposes some of the hidden modes of African-American communities which have transformed both African retentions and Euro-American realities into a way of survival. Although my treatment of the full implications of Williams's theory has been necessarily cursory here, I use it to show how women writers are "mothering" the residual into the emergent—constructing knowledge while deconstructing oppositions.

In presenting the dialectics of residual African-based culture and constantly emerging African-American society, authors Walker, Morrison and Marshall (re)define their culture in broad diasporal strokes, uncovering aspects of their communal heritage veiled by hegemonic dominant discourse. In *The Signifying Monkey*, Henry Louis Gates, Jr. calls this practice a "self-reflective" tradition, "reassembling the fragments [of the diaspora] that contain the traces of a coherent system of order" (xxiv). Gates examines this tradition in terms of language and the signifyin(g) of the [mostly male] trickster; here I examine another aspect of (re)-asssemblage—the telling of the tales through a gynocentric mothering process. Both in the stories they tell and in the telling itself, the women writers examined here continue the line of African and African-American women storytellers who pass on the message of their culture to future generations. These writers not only (re)-assemble the fragments of the past by rendering "implicit as explicit" (Gates xxiv), but dialectically they turn the vision on itself and render it implicit again. To foreground discussion of the African-American writers, it may be useful to address cursorily the estrangement from and (self)discovery of African heritage for Black Americans.

Dialogue on Africa and one's own African heritage has been prominent in the course of African-American history. Views toward African retentions have ranged from E. Franklin Frazier's, "But, of the habits and customs as well as the hopes and fears that characterized the life of their forebears in Africa, nothing remains," to modern scholars such as Joyce Ladner's view that African survivalisms have integrally shaped Black American family and culture.[13] Depending on the historical moment and the identity of the major writers and spokespersons at the time, one side of the conflicting dialectics—the desire to assimilate or to assert one's own ethnic identity—has been stronger. It has been conjectured that had the Africans truly assimilated into American culture, they would have quickly lost these residual practices, but this view may in fact be a limiting vision of the complex working of culture. During the Harlem Renaissance and in the 1960s as well as at the present time, emergent movements have been concerned with the identification of one's African roots. But even when the historicity of the age compelled an assimilationist stance as dominant action, within communities African cultural practices remained alternative practice.

Throughout generations and varying political movements, Black women have continued the alternative practice of passing on the cultural values of their African forebears to their children—even when they did not recognize these cultural values as "African"—so that the unique qualities of their heritage have not been lost. This attention to maintaining one's cultural identity has shown up repeatedly in the writings of twentieth-century Black women writers. Hurston evoked the meaning of "Africa" found within the rich folklife of the African-American community rather than idealized Africa as exotica, as sentimentalists such as Langston Hughes, Countee Cullen, and Claude McKay had done.[14] Alice Walker, who identifies herself as Hurston's literary descendant, comments on what she sees as a distinct difference between Black male and female writers, and she examines why the writings by Black men have perhaps not always addressed the Black community. She feels that these writings tend to focus less on the Black family and community than on "white people as primary antagonists. The consequences of this is [*sic*] that many of our books by 'major' writers (always male) tell us little about the culture, history, or future, imagination, fantasies, and so on, of black people" (*In Search of Our Mothers' Gardens* 261–62). Walker further remarks that it is women who are, in Efua Sutherland's words, "minding the culture" and who have kept the traditions and uniqueness of African-American life alive.

Although many African retentions have been noted in African-American life, from agriculture and food practices to music and religion, I concentrate on areas germane to this study: the survival of the African family organization, community patterns, oral traditions, and the role of women in passing on the traditions of their culture. Although the unique quality of Black family organization has been seen by hegemonic white sociologists as pathological since it deviates from the supposed norm of the "mainstream" nuclear family structure, there is increased documentation to tie this extended family system to African family patterns.[15] In response to "pathology" theorists, historian Sudarkasa comments that what has been seen as instability in marital (conjugal) relations is actually a stability in kinship (consanguinal) ties: "Even though the constraints of slavery did prohibit the replication of African lineage . . . the extended family networks that were formed during slavery by Africans *and their descendants* were based on the institutional heritage which the Africans had brought with them to this continent" (39–45). Sudarkasa emphasizes the notion of collectivity as part of this extended structure, whether it was familial or community-based. Under the violent constraints of slavery, many variations of these family structures appeared, since biological families were split apart and sold. However, consanguinal kin attempted to keep track of those parents, children, siblings, aunts, and uncles lost, and against tremendous odds, sought to reconnect with them after the demise of slavery. Whether consanguinal or communal, extended units often continued, with—as in matrifocal African cultures—the mother as central figure.

The role of the mothering members of the African-American extended family—the biological mother, grandmother, older aunt, and female ancestor—is integral to the discussion of the texts in the African-American section of this book. A major function within this role emphasizes the socialization of children as well as the passing on of heritage to the community. La Frances Rodgers-Rose, in "The Black Woman: A Historical Overview," identifies the Black woman in terms of her role in preserving African heritage and retaining African values and practices:

> She survived the long middle passage from Africa to America, bringing with her many of the diverse characteristics of her African mothers. . . . She gave her children love, cooked for them, protected them, *told them about life, about freedom, about survival, about loving, about pain, about joy and about Africa.* (9–10; emphasis added)

The Black woman has been seen not only as the central link in Black family organization but as one individual who fought to keep any semblance of family together in opposition to racism and oppression. But this vision has also been problematic for women's growth. The stereotypic image of the Black woman as "matriarch" or "superwoman" has often left little room for attention to women's own needs and desires. The strength of Black women derived from their African heritage—within a Christian Euro-American hegemony which envisions women as weak—has often been viewed negatively by both the dominant culture and by men in Black culture.[16] Therefore, their important position in the Black community has been compromised by the historicity of American experience. At the same time, African-American women, like their African sisters, have also been limited by some of the African-based values they pass on. As part of a tradition derived from Africa, the mother, grandmother, or older female relative taught their children about the environment and passed on stories from the past (individual achievements, collective history, and folk tales echoing the African-woman-storyteller's voice). Therefore, the emphasis on having children to pass on the values and traditions of the culture has been paramount in African-American communities as well. According to Ladner, "The ultimate test of womanhood, then, is one's ability to bring forth life. This value underlying childbearing is much akin to the traditional way in which the same behavior has been perceived in African culture" (212). For both African and African-American women, the emphasis on childbearing and rearing causes both conflict and fulfillment, as examination of the texts reveals. In spite of the connectedness and power gained from one's heritage, women still suffer the limitations handed down from their African forebears, compounded by the otherness of being Black and female in a patriarchal, Euro-American society. Aware of these contradictions, the writers discussed here still perceive the relationship of children to their extended family and the community as essential for the life and health of the children themselves, but they envision a broad definition of children—their own and their readers'. Their texts are informed by a consciousness of what must be passed on to future generations; the telling of the tale is paramount to the survival of the culture. Like their African sister-storytellers, these writers create oraliterature in their written works.

They (re)assemble the fragmented sounds of their foremothers' voices, rendering explicit the implicit memory of African orature.

## IV.

"Mothers handing down the future to their daughters" is how Nigerian novelist Buchi Emecheta defines "generational continuity" in *Our Own Freedom* (47). It is the cultural traditions and education which have been handed down from grandmother to grandchild across time and the Atlantic to foster both modern African and African-American cultures. What we see from the voices of these Black women writers is that their concerns may not be entirely different from those of their male counterparts in wanting to communicate a message, liberate and bolster their own people, and improve their society; but in the manner of production and the focus of the material, these women writers have a distinguishable aim. They address the formerly unvoiced members of the community—the wife, the barren woman, the young child, the mother, the grandmother. They look at their existence as a continuum, an invisible thread drawn through the women's stories to women readers and the men who will listen. Through their alternative, mothering practice, these writers (re)construct residual herstory as emergent culture.

# I

## The
## Africans

# 1

## Flora Nwapa,
## *Efuru*

> "The rearing of a child," the Igbo say, "is
> not a job for one person nor is a child a
> child for only one person."
>
> Kamene Okonjo

■ Flora Nwapa's first novel, *Efuru* (1966), is a fitting start-
ing point for an examination of the integral relationship between
women's role in the oral tradition and the oraliterature that African
women create. Nwapa is Nigeria's first woman novelist and the first
African woman writer to publish a novel in English; moreover, her
depiction of village women's lives reflects the orature which informs
all the works in this study. With the publication of *Efuru*, Flora
Nwapa brought a fresh perspective to traditional West African culture and modern Nigeria in literary works by exploring a woman's
point of view and exposing a society close to its precolonial roots.
She has been widely praised for her ability in adapting English to
capture the flavor of the Igbo language. Her use of the oral tradition
and folk idiom underscores the concept of generational continuity
and reflects a commitment to pass on the orature of her foremothers
in her writings. Nwapa tells us that she "writes stories about women
because these stories are familiar to her. . . . It's left to the critics to
say if I write for the women of Nigeria or if I write for all African
women. I think of the story and I think of how best to write the
story."[1] Despite her disclaimer, Nwapa writes for and about African
women, their past life and their present, bringing their stories to
future generations; moreover, she writes her "stories" with a "keen

ear for village voices" (Emenyonu 31) and with an oraliterary form, based on the tales she heard as a child.

Although most critics point to Nwapa's startling ability to recreate the voices of her village women, not all perceive this as an achievement. Eustace Palmer, cited as a "Eurocentric" African critic by the authors of *Toward the Decolonization of African Literature*,[2] denigrates Nwapa as a weak imitation of her male counterparts. He states in a derogatory manner what might be praise from an Afrocentric critic: "It is as if Flora Nwapa has set herself the task of writing an East Nigerian epic and wants to ensure, whatever the subject matter, her novel should embody the culture and spirit of her tribe" (57). What Palmer fails to realize is that Nwapa's subject matter—the place of women in a communal village society—is inextricable from her representation of the culture and its oral traditions. In this examination of *Efuru*, I explore how Nwapa embodies the "culture and spirit of her tribe" through the eyes and voices of the village women. Nwapa's writings reveal her debt to the orature of her culture, women's place in that culture, and the importance of women's role in passing on cultural values to future generations. In her work, Nwapa illustrates dialectically that, as upholders of tradition, women are powerful figures, economically secure and socially vibrant, yet they are limited in their choices by the restrictive cultural milieu. In examining this women-centered, Afrocentric literature, we witness how Nwapa, as African woman storyteller, passes on her cultural history to generations of modern African women; moreover, the exploration of African communal values, encoded in women's voices, sets the groundwork for discussion in the African-American section, particularly Alice Walker's Southern recreation of an African village compound in *The Color Purple*.

In the introduction I referred to the appalling lack of documentation concerning the role of women in the oral tradition. As only the master (male) chefs are accounted for in terms of cuisine, so only the "master" storytellers have been acknowledged; however, in every village compound and every kitchen, this creative folk art has been performed by women as well. In commenting on her use of women's stories that are "familiar to her," Nwapa reflects a tradition in which the telling of the tale, its repetition, and its alteration, are based on generational continuity, mutual historicity, and shared cultural values. Emmanuel Obiechina, in his study of oral tradition in West African novels, explains: "Oral cultures are relatively more homogeneous than literate cultures because oral transmission depends on face-to-face contact and ensures common customs, beliefs, techniques, sentiments and general outlook" (32). Unfortunately, Obiechina does not explore these possibilities in any women writers, but *Efuru*, as a written response to an oral form, has the orality of Igbo culture inscribed in the writing.

In an insightful study, *Women Writers in Black Africa*, Lloyd Brown comments on Nwapa: "In evoking the style of oral literature, the novelist incorporates into her own narrative those indigenous traditions which the style represents" (141). Brown has touched on a major tenet in Nwapa's style, but I think this position can be taken one step further. More than a stylistic choice by a novelist, this form represents *precisely* women's role in the community to maintain the cultural and moral order of the society; in writing about village women, and as a woman herself, Nwapa pays deserved attention to her artistic predecessors—village mothers and grandmothers who have passed on the knowledge of their culture through their stories, songs, tales, and proverbs. (Alice Walker's vision of Phillis Wheatley's mother in *In Search of Our Mothers' Gardens* comes straight from Nwapa's village women.) Whether from her own mother's tales or the stories told at twilight by the women in her compound and community, Nwapa's foremothers informed her creative art. It is not a coincidence that Nwapa writes women-centered literature or that her literature has a predominantly oral form.

Whether negatively, "The dialogue seldom rises above the level of women's gossip" (Lindfors, "Achebe's Followers" 577) or positively, "Talk, more specifically the talk of women, establishes the [cultural] milieu" (Brown, *Women Writers of Black Africa* 137), Nwapa's critics have generally agreed on one aspect of her work— her attention to the sounds and voices of women. Nwapa has excelled in her ability to capture spoken Igbo language within the context of written English; she has also linked this linguistic device to the content of her novel. The orality of her language is exhibited in the structure of the novel by the extensive use of dialogue, the way information is communicated, and the use of folk tales, stories, and proverbs as methods of initiation and instruction within the context of the novel—and for the reader as well. Nwapa's writing style is unique in that it is rarely descriptive and always understated; the information we receive is passed on to us by dialogue as it is to the other characters, particularly the village women. Although the narration strikes one cursorily as omniscient, it is actually a collective narrative of these community women through the voice of the story-teller. The sounds of the women—some sweet, some discordant—constantly structure and restructure the pattern of village life, and eventually all information, whether wanted or not, is shared.

Equally, *Efuru*'s narrative structure appears deceptively simple. The plot concerns Efuru, a remarkable woman who marries two worthless men of her own choosing, against the strictures of the community. Being childless most of her life and without a biological context for marriage, Efuru finally becomes a worshipper of the lake deity, Uhamiri. Beneath this apparently unembellished story, based on a popular African folk tale (which I discuss in detail later in the chapter), is a complex exploration and critique of a traditional West African culture and the role of women in these societies. *Efuru* takes place in village compounds, markets, and streams, and at these gatherings, the social and moral behavior of members of the community is the constant base of discourse. M. M. Green cites this aspect of women's responsibilities in her study of Igbo village women: "Any type of gathering could be used for discussing and restating the ethical standards of the community" (186). Revealingly, the voice of the community that demands adherence to strict social codes for its women most often comes from the women themselves. The paradox of this system, adding to the complexity of linguistical meaning in the novel, is that women often uphold traditions and practices which limit their choices and rights as women. In a vivid example early on in the novel, Efuru faces this conflict when speaking with the woman practitioner whom her mother-in-law has brought to give Efuru her "bath" (an Igbo term for female circumcision). In the conversation between the three women, the practitioner performing the circumcision initiates Efuru into the world of women as well as warns her of the disasters of those who do not follow the traditions:

> "You are the young wife, my daughter. You are beautiful my daughter. I will be gentle with you. Don't be afraid. It is painful no doubt, but the pain disappears like hunger. You know what?" and she turned to Efuru's mother-in-law. "You know Nwakaego's daughter?"
> "Yes, I know her."

"She did not have her bath before she had that baby who died
after that dreadful flood."

"God forbid. Why?"

"Fear. She was afraid. Foolish girl. She had a foolish mother,
their folly cost them a son, a good son." (10)

From this passage we can see several ways in which Nwapa
evokes the dilemma of female circumcision by utilizing the orality of
the traditional culture. I examine Nwapa's use of proverbs in more
detail shortly, but the significance of this speech form in Igbo culture is evident in the passage. The woman practitioner who is there
to help Efuru through the pain of circumcision does so by offering a
proverb: "The pain disappears like hunger." The teaching of the
tradition is passed on to the younger generation through an everyday speech sprinkled with proverbs and aphorisms. Also included in
this passage is a reference to the exigency of women in passing down
these customs to protect the younger ones as well as a caveat concerning the consequences of not listening to the wisdom of the
elders. The anecdote of the young girl who would not submit to her
"bath" and loses her child is told to strengthen Efuru's resolve;
moreover, it is a comment on how the young woman was not taught
the traditions correctly—not only is she foolish, but so is her mother
who allowed her to give in to her fears. Yet, this is also a telling
example where women uphold a tradition—circumcision—which
can be harmful to the women themselves. The young woman, in this
case, Efuru, does not speak of her fear or her resistance to this
painful ordeal; she is silenced by the older woman's warning of the
possibility of disaster if she disobeys. The language itself covers up
the action and, thus, the orature does not necessarily protect the
women but reinforces a practice basically antithetical to women's
health and desires.

As noted in the discussion above, the linguistical content of the
dialogue is imbued with communal folk references and oral wisdom,
particularly through the use of proverbs. Everyday speech is often
formalized to presentments. To back up any moral judgment, the
speaker will exclaim, "our people say" or "our fathers say." This last
phrase may appear to be in opposition to the premise that it is
women who pass on cultural mores; rather, since men are often the
ones formulating many of these values, the ancestors may also be

"generically" seen as male (of course). Another use of language as folk wisdom is in the process of naming. When Efuru's only daughter dies from convulsions, the neighbors sympathize with her by referring to this process: "'Our people call their children: Onwuamaegbu'—Death does not know how to kill, and 'Onwuzurigbo'—Death is universal. So take heart, my daughter'" (116). Most importantly, the use of proverbs in the narrative mirrors their significance in an African oral culture; proverbs are interwoven with ordinary speech and exist as part of the spoken language. As in the passage above, even names can be proverbs, so tied are these linguistic forms to the communication process. The majority of proverbs in the novel refer to family relations and the continuity of the past, present, and future, and they reinforce relevant contextual aspects of the narrative. One proverb revealingly demonstrates the importance of looking into family background before choosing a mate: "The son of the gorilla must dance like the father gorilla" (59). Another proverb emphasizes the primacy of marriage as well as women's secondary position in the social sphere: "Di bu mma ogori" (119; "A husband makes a woman beautiful"). One final example illustrates the generalization of tomorrow as an unknown entity but also demonstrates how matrifocal the culture is: "Tomorrow is pregnant as we say" (165).

Nwapa's incorporation of the orature of her culture into her narrative discourse centers on one folk tale, told in its entirety in chapter 7. This is the popular folk tale of the beautiful, proud girl who will not marry anyone her parents pick for her but chooses a handsome stranger instead. It is one of the most potent African moral tales regarding women's behavior and is recounted in many forms; it features in such written literature as diverse as Amos Tutuola's *The Palm-Wine Drinkard* and J. P. Clark's *The Masquerade*. There are many versions of this tale, but whether the handsome stranger the young girl follows turns into a python, a spirit, or a skull, her decision ends in disaster. This tale has had a profound effect on many African women writers, and each of the chapters in this section contains one work which uses this tale as a central metaphor. In *Efuru*, the tale is analogous to the broader aims of the narrative. First, the dramatic presentation of the folk tale takes place in Efuru's compound. Although the "master" storyteller in this instance is male, it is Efuru who has organized the occasion, and the children flock to her compound to listen to a night of folk stories.

Efuru, known for her patience, goodness, and suffering, becomes a communal mother for the children after the death of her only daughter. Although the children have heard the tale many times, they beg to hear it again: "'Tell us about the woman whose daughter disobeyed her and as a result was married to a spirit'" (131). As evidence of the profound role of the mother in society, the children see the central character as the mother who was disobeyed rather than the daughter who follows the spirit. Moreover, the tale's content mirrors other aspects of the novel's plot. The tale is used to instruct young girls to be humble and to obey their families. This tale has special meaning for Efuru. Unlike the mother in the tale, Efuru's mother is dead and not able to advise her in life; like this proud young woman, however, Efuru does not listen to her father or her aunts and marries whom she chooses.

In Igbo communities, as in African cultures in general, the choosing of a husband or wife is a lengthy process which involves the entire extended family. In Victor Uchendu's study of Igbo culture, he states that marriage is viewed as "an alliance between two families instead of between two people" (50). Uchendu emphatically sets down the necessity of the parents' and extended family's role in the choice of a mate. Therefore, Efuru's elopement with her first husband, Adizua, can be seen as an act in total opposition to her family and tradition. And, like the girl's choice in the folk tale, hers ends in disaster. Nwapa, as the authorial voice, appears to place no blame on Efuru for her choices; rather, she calls Efuru a "remarkable" woman for choosing her first husband without worrying about the consequences (1). Yet, Efuru's marriages to two irresponsible husbands whom she chooses without consulting her family or looking into their family backgrounds, as well as the discourse surrounding this folk tale, suggest that Nwapa is unresolved about the possibility of a successful marriage without the advice of the elders. The conflict between a Western-style approach to women's marital and family relations versus the security and stability of an African traditional system reflects a tension which runs throughout the novel. Clearly, this tension is articulated in the novel's attention to the education of children. Often there is a conflict as to what the woman in the community wishes for herself and what she is mandated to pass on to the children. For, as Igbo sociologist Ada Mere notes, women are the "most primary and constant agents of child socialization" (4). The child is central to this matrifocal culture that Nwapa writes about, and the woman—mother, grandmother, aunt, older sister—is the link between the child and the community. Nwapa's novel, as woman-centered oraliterature, focuses not merely on woman's position as wife and mother, but on her role in child-socialization and its implications for the community as a whole. The women instruct all children, both male and female, in learning the values of the culture up to a certain age. Donatus Nwoga, philosopher and critic, remarks that at age thirteen, the boys in most West African cultures are separated and educated by the men while the girls remain under the women's domain. I mentioned earlier that although the women are in charge of the education and initiation of young girls into adulthood, they are not always free to teach what they would like. As upholders of the traditions, they are compelled to act "in line with past practice" (Abrahams 4) whether they agree with the custom or not. In a dual sex role culture, this aspect of women's responsibility is one which demands great respect from the society, yet the contradictions inherent in what *they* teach reflect the perceived oppositions in Nwapa's discourse. Furthermore, the importance of childbearing in relation to child rearing is a major source of contention in the novel.

In *Efuru*, there are many references to child socialization. From the "training" of Ogea, the young woman who lives with Efuru, and the passing on of tales as a method of instruction to Efuru's aunt Ajanupu's constant lecturing, women keep watch over all the children of the community (even if these "children" are technically adults). Yet, throughout the novel, Efuru often behaves in a manner which seems to circumvent daily customs and the women's advice. Although she appears to respect the traditions, she often seeks her own way. A far-reaching example of her actions is one already mentioned: Efuru alone chooses both husbands and marries the first without the bride price being paid (1). Other examples include her less-than-strict attitude toward Ogea's upbringing and her decision not to farm with her husband Adizua as he asks but rather to trade in town (18). Efuru is a very independent and headstrong character. Part of her independence comes from a traditional aspect of her community; as Nwapa notes, the Oguta women "are very industrious; women are the live wire of the whole place" (11 July 1983). But Efuru appears more independent than many of the other women of her village, Oguta. The relationship of the individual to the community, explored in much African literature, takes on an added dimension when the individual is a woman. One possible reason for Efuru's lack of compliance with the traditions of her culture may come from a lack of maternal guidance during her childhood. Efuru's mother died when Efuru was very young, and being the only child of a favorite wife, she was doted on by her father. Another reason for her independence may be her association with the lake deity, Uhamiri, whose relationship with Efuru is examined later in this chapter. Efuru's independence of spirit has both positive and negative effects on her life. Like Nwapa, Efuru is a "remarkable" woman, yet her headstrong nature leads her to pick two worthless husbands.

Maryse Condé comments that "although [Efuru] shows such determination, she still remains strongly attached to traditions" (135). Although Condé perceives this attachment to traditions as solely restrictive, the novel's discourse presents the traditions dialectically—they both hamper and sustain Efuru. Even though she is independent, Efuru does not live outside society. And it is her Igbo society which has created an environment to foster her strength, resourcefulness, and goodness, but which has also determined that Efuru cannot fulfill her primary role in society because she is childless. Since the death of her only daughter, she has not been able to conceive another child. Like her mother before her, she had only one child, a girl, but Efuru's child died. Since the "primary purpose of the Igbo marriage is to raise a family" (Okonkwo 145), the childless Efuru cannot be what society expects of her, nor can she fulfill herself within that context. No matter how good a marriage is, the culture says, it means nothing unless there are children to show for it. Sociologist Ada Mere expressed this concept to me in an interview: "In a pro-natalist society, marriage is the expected end; when procreation doesn't happen, that woman has failed an essential life goal" (25 April 1984). Efuru is painfully aware of her inability to conform to society, and in thinking about her problem she reiterates Mere's statement: "It was a curse not to have children. Her people did not take it as one of the numerous accidents of nature. It was regarded as a failure" (207).

The issue of the failure of the childless woman is explored in a more somber manner in Nwapa's second novel, *Idu,* but the implications are equally clear in this novel: Efuru is a "remarkable" woman, but she cannot pass on her goodness to her child (Scheub 552). In a community that believes in the spiritual/genetic passage of values through kinship lines as well as environmental instruction, childlessness amounts to a cultural tragedy. A younger generation must continue the lineage from ancestors to descendants, and the community needs to people future generations. For the community, Efuru's happy marriage with second husband, Eneberi, cannot mitigate her infertility. In the following passage, we hear the voices of the community women speaking of Efuru's barrenness while they wash clothes at the stream. This passage emphasizes not only the importance of having a child but also the community's demand for it. Again, the women are often the most pitiless in protecting the traditions from which they do not always benefit. The attitude and conflict presented here also surfaces in Aidoo's *Dilemma of a Ghost* (chapter 3). The community women comment:

> "Seeing them together is not the important thing," another said. "The important thing is that nothing has happened since the happy marriage. We are not going to eat happy marriage. Marriage must be fruitful. Of what use is it if it is not fruitful. Of what use is it if your husband licks your body, worships you and buys everything in the market for you and you are not productive?" (171)

As upholders of the tradition, women can be the harshest critics of those who cannot conform to a conventional role. They are caught in a bind because many of the traditions are not to women's best advantage, yet they must honor them. In the above passage, we witness a lack of sympathy for Efuru's predicament by the main speaker, Omirima. And even though we might assume that—as a woman—the speaker would be more understanding, clearly she feels her duty to function as the voice of community authority as well. She sees herself as the mouthpiece of community demands when she says: "'*We* are not going to eat happy marriage'" (171). In this case, Omirima represents a most obdurate custodian of cultural mores, as does her sister-figure in *Idu*, Onyemuru. The voices of these community women are sometimes harsh, other times sympathetic, but the traditional culture which has given them a powerful voice in the decisions of the society also limits their choices.

The textural background of the novel is the constant discourse of the community women, advising, instructing, commenting, sympathizing, gossiping. The sounds of men are eclipsed by the overflow of female voices. As Carole Boyce Davies notes in "Motherhood in the Works of Male and Female Igbo Writers": "The author creates a world of women; men are shown as intruders" (249). These female voices are a community chorus and reflect the collective narration. The concept of a collective female chorus is prevalent in African orature; moreover, it is evident in much women's literature and surfaces strongly in both African and African-American women's writings. The collective talk, as part of this oral structure, shares an expressive body of knowledge and values. Indeed, the talk in this novel ranges from medicinal cures and advising children to malicious gossip. Talk also "influences personal attitudes and social relationships by reenacting pertinent experiences" and determines "judgment by offering clues to the speaker's moral character" (Brown 137), as well as the characters of those spoken about! Most importantly, the context of this talk is a communal language which is on a continuum from the past into the future. It is part of an oral art form which Obiechina defines as embodying the "collective outlook and ethics" of its culture. Although Obiechina is referring to the more consciously artistic aspects of oral culture, the passage certainly applies to the predominance of formalized talk in this novel. When the community women speak, they do so as a group, emphasizing their "collective outlook." For example, when Efuru returns to her father's house after her first husband has left her, the women of her own village comfort her in this manner:

> "Efuru, the daughter of Nwashike Ogene, welcome to your father's house. You did well, my daughter. We are sorry that your husband had rubbed charcoal on your face, but we are glad that you have left him to come back to us. We women married to men of your village are very happy, so when we see women of your village ill-treated by their husbands, we feel it very keenly. You have done well to come back. You are young, beautiful and of good parentage, so you will soon have a good husband." (110)

As I have noted previously, there is a formal structure to the language, based on choric repetition and alteration. In addition, shared assumptions within the passage allow the speaker to use the pronoun "we" instead of "I." Values of community are stressed, for the ideal structure for all village societies is "harmony and integration," as playwright 'Zulu Ṣofọla, has remarked. From the above passage, it is clear that everyone in Efuru's village knows exactly what happened to her. The concept of "mind your own business" does not exist in this village setting. Whether true or not, there is a communal agreement that the women of this village are happy with their lives and do not wish to see a relative of their men mistreated.[3] Finally, they all concur on Efuru's future: Not only is she young and beautiful, but she comes from a good family and therefore will get a good husband. As Juliet Okonkwo notes in her article on Igbo marriage, great care is taken to look at the blood relatives of the prospective mate to make sure they are "okay" (141).

Two women of the community bear special mention because they illustrate the worst and best qualities of this communal system. One is Omirima, a malicious gossip, whose voice we have already heard. The other is Ajanupu, Efuru's aunt-in-law and confidante. Omirima's overbearing voice is at once comical and malevolent as she speaks for the community's demands. Any child in the community, be it Efuru herself or Efuru's unborn child, is under Omirima's authority. In another example, when Omirima interferes with the family's process of finding another wife for Efuru's second husband, Eneberi, she uses her kinship ties to get in the last word. When Efuru's mother-in-law asks Omirima why she is being so "vehement" about Efuru's barrenness, Omirima answers: "'In other words you are saying that I have no right to discuss it. You talk like a child. You forget our relationship. You forget that my great grandfather and your grandmother had the same father. *So Eneberi is my son, as well as yours*'" (230; emphasis added). Omirima clearly identifies herself as part of an extended family in which she, as an elder "mother," has the right to give advice and make judgments. Omirima is constantly the source of bad news, and her position as elder woman and ethical advisor is used solely to enforce demands, spread vicious rumors, and denigrate others in the community. The attitude of most of the villagers toward Omirima is summed up by Efuru's niece Ogea: "'She has never in her life said anything good about anybody. I wonder who is going to be her next victim'" (244).

In contrast, Efuru's Aunt Ajanupu illustrates the beneficial aspects of this communal system. Although equally overbearing, she is a generous woman and has the good of Efuru and the community at heart. Although she is the aunt of Efuru's first husband, she never deserts Efuru, even after Efuru marries a second time. When Ogonim, Efuru's only child, dies, Ajanupu controls the women sympathizers and runs the household (89–91). Later she advises

Efuru to choose a second wife for Eneberi when it is clear that Efuru will have no more children (206). Although Ajanupu might wish otherwise, she understands the community's demand for children and helps Efuru to choose the wife before Eneberi and his mother pick someone Efuru might find objectionable. Unlike Omirima, who often uses the communal system to her own vicious ends, Ajanupu has one eye on the traditions and the other on the welfare of the younger women.

With the help of her advisor Ajanupu, Efuru tries to fit into the prescribed conventions of society. But she can no longer remain married after her second husband accuses her of adultery while she is gravely ill. Ajanupu, as maintainer of the traditions, curses Eneberi, "'Our ancestors will punish you,'" because he should know that Efuru's marital fidelity is passed down through her female ancestors (275). Efuru is shocked and insulted at his accusation; she decides to give up living with men and accept the fate chosen for her. She explains the situation after returning to her father's village: "'Then a rumor went round that I was guilty of adultery—My mother was not an adulterous woman, neither was her mother, why should I be different? Was it possible to learn to be left-handed at old age?'" (279). For Efuru, fidelity is a value passed down through genera-tions of women just as learning to cook food a certain way is taught from mother to daughter. Intangible values and life choices are part of the cultural heritage that is passed down from the ancestors.

It is Efuru's biological fate not to conform to women's pre-scribed role; moreover, it may also be her spiritual destiny, stem-ming from her association with the woman of the lake, Uhamiri. Uhamiri is a very important deity to the people of Efuru's commu-nity because she presides over the large lake that lies at the edge of the village. Uhamiri, the owner of the lake, blesses the community with fish and fresh water and brings them wealth and beauty. Nwapa's own fascination with Oguta's woman of the lake shows up in most of her writing, specifically in her children's book, *Mammy Water*. Efuru's relationship with Uhamiri develops gradually. She accepts her destiny as worshipper rather late in the novel, yet the people of the area start to make connections between Efuru and the deity much earlier. One of the first descriptions of Efuru's physical appearance is given to us by a farmer. In exclaiming about her great beauty, he says, "'You would think that the woman of the lake is her mother'" (8). Efuru is also known to be a very kind, fair, and resourceful woman. These qualities, too, are believed to come from the benevolent water spirit, Uhamiri. When Efuru starts to have dreams about a woman under the water who invites her to share kola, she goes to her father and narrates her dream: "'The old man laughed softly. "Your dream is good. The woman of the lake, our Uhamiri, has chosen you to be one of her worshippers. . . . Your mother had similar dreams" (182). Just as Efuru's fidelity to her husbands and to marriage in general has been passed down through her female predecessors, her consanguinity to Uhamiri is also part of this heritage from her mother. Yet this blessing is also a curse for Efuru. In Igbo cosmology, the deity Uhamiri can grant women wealth but never children.[4] Ironically, although Uhamiri brings fertility to both the land and water, she is unable to bring fertility to women. Omirima, mortified that the childless Efuru is considering becoming a worshipper of Uhamiri, sneers to Eneberi's mother: "'How many women in this town who worship Uhamiri have children? Your daughter-in-law must be a foolish woman to go into that. Amede, you are to blame. . . . You are the mother, why didn't you point this out to her?'" (203). Efuru herself questions Uhamiri's strength since the woman of the lake is unable to help her get what she most wants—a child: "It struck her that since she has started to worship Uhamiri, she had never seen babies in her abode. 'Can she give me children? . . . She cannot give me children because she has got no children herself'" (207–208). Efuru, aware of what becoming a worshipper might mean, is reticent about her association with the deity, but eventually she comes to accept it. Chinua Achebe, discussing Efuru's decision to become a worshipper with me, commented that she was specially chosen by Uhamiri: "Well, she didn't choose that; it's not everyone who can do that. The god chooses you. That was a case where even the childlessness, the problems were instigated by the god" (personal interview, 7 March 1984). Beyond representing an aspect of Igbo religion, Efuru's association with Uhamiri may also be seen as a microcosm of women's relationship to the traditional society in general. Her place as priestess of Uhamiri gives her great strength and power, yet it stops her from totally fulfilling her role as a woman in Igbo society. In the same way, the traditional culture gives women strength and power in passing on the traditions, yet these same traditions limit their roles.

The acceptance of the personal relationship of human to deity, as shown in *Efuru*, reflects the world view explored in oraliterature. According to Obiechina, "The supernatural has a stronger hold on the oral tradition than on the literate tradition. . . . The representation of reality within the rural novels takes account of the traditional world view. This does not divide the universe rigidly into the spiritual and the non-spiritual" (33; 37). Within the context of *Efuru*'s world view, Efuru finds herself a niche to remain a vibrant member of the community without disrupting the society; she becomes a worshipper of the woman of the lake, the deity Uhamiri. Although Efuru's choice is not open to all women, her acceptance of her role as one of Uhamiri's worshippers does offer an option for Igbo women who bear fruit other than children. I have noted that Nwapa is writing woman-centered literature, and clearly, her use of a female deity as a moving force in the novel is an excellent example of it. Sylvia Leith-Ross suggests in her study of Igbo village women that men are less likely to approach the deity of earth and fertility, Ajala, because they feel that women are closer to her, "being women together" (117). This vision of spirituality underscores male-female relations in Nwapa's novel generally. The dual sex role system of precolonial Africa remains fairly intact in Nwapa's 1940s Igbo village. The community women control a large part of the society, the domestic sphere, and through the having and instructing of children, they set up a system of passing on cultural values which is woman-dominated. Unfortunately, in Efuru's limited position, she is unable to fulfill one of the main roles demanded of her. In her immediate line, the wives deliver only female children, and her daughter has died. So, it is through her association with Uhamiri that Efuru fulfills an alternative, woman-centered function in the society.

Efuru places her mark on the community in two ways—as a priestess for Uhamiri and as a communal mother to the children around her. In this way, she joins the collective chorus of women. Although she cannot pass on her goodness and special powers to a daughter, she can use her role as a woman worshipper to interpret the deity Uhamiri to her fellow community members. Efuru's prosperity as a trader and her kindness bring wealth and beauty to the community, and with her as a worshipper, Uhamiri will look kindly on her people. For those who live by the lake, Efuru is the human counterpart of Uhamiri. Through her position as worshipper, she substantiates her earlier work in the community, and her good qualities will be passed on to those she helps. The novel suggests that Efuru's benevolence comes from this spiritual source. She treats all the other villagers as members of her extended family, but because of her personal loss, her characteristic strength and goodness pour out specifically to the children.

This chapter opened with a proverb which stated that the upbringing of children belongs to the whole community as well as to the parents. Since Efuru is childless, this system allows her to behave as a communal mother after her only child dies. She loves children, and they are always around her compound. There are nights of storytelling, and she is constantly in tune with the games the children around her are playing. Efuru assists in the delivery of Eneberi's second wife's child and later becomes the primary mother to that child (261). She takes care of Ogea's brothers and sisters when they are visiting, and she is always looking after the children of her confidante, Ajanupu. Efuru shares her food not only with the children of her friends but with any child who enters her compound. These small incidents give us insight into Efuru's communal mothering and point to the poignant, unresolved ending of the novel: As Efuru surrenders herself to Uhamiri, she dreams of the woman of the lake who is beautiful, rich, and happy, but who can have no children. Efuru thinks: "She [Uhamiri] had never experienced the joys of motherhood. Why then did the women worship her?" (281). This line has been read tragically by critics and also cited as Nwapa's inability to resolve her subject and take a stand. But in the context of the novel, we see Efuru coming to terms with her biological fate and still managing to keep her rightful place in society. In this way, *Efuru* takes a radical stance: Yes, a woman can be childless and still be valuable to her society. The ending itself may be unresolved because Efuru's choice also comes with loss or because Nwapa may be ending the novel in the manner of a dilemma tale (which I examine more fully in chapter 3)—we as readers are left to question Efuru's society as Nwapa does.

In this chapter on Flora Nwapa's *Efuru*, I have examined aspects of women's role in Igbo community life, particularly their function as maintainers of the traditions and the conflicts that arise from this responsibility. I have also underscored the orality of Nwapa's writing in that the author, in the manner of her foremothers, formulates her novel as oraliterature, relying on the undocumented orature of village women. Nwapa's attention to the details of daily life expose us to the heart of "the culture and spirit of her tribe." Nwapa not only explores the passing on of cultural traditions through the female members of her Igbo community, she also passes on the history and culture of an almost precolonial traditional West African village to those of her readers who remember and those who have never known it. As a woman writer, Nwapa reflects her traditional role in African culture in a broad, literary sense: Through her novels and children's stories, she passes on the life of her culture. And this Afrocentric, woman-centered literature reflects the aims of the African-American writers discussed in the second section; the story-telling traditions and the values of community life that Nwapa re-cords are threads that run throughout the diaspora and this book.

# 2

## Efua Sutherland,
## *Foriwa*

> I've heard a lot of people discussing at con-
> ferences the role of the [African] writer—all
> this rigmarole, well if there's any role, they
> should write *for the children*.
>
> Efua Sutherland

■ In *Efuru* and her other works, Flora Nwapa examines the relationship of the individual to the community from a woman's perspective. The discourse of her novels concerns the tensions between women's power base in the traditional community and the limitations imposed on them. How women negotiate their position in traditional and changing African cultures is directly tied to the oral traditions which they maintain. Chapter 1 focused on Nwapa's recording of her culture's life through the undocumented orature of village women and the traditions they pass on to the next generation. In this chapter, I focus on Efua Sutherland's intention to take a more activist role than Nwapa in recording her culture's traditions and women's role in them. Sutherland's aim is to transform these traditions so that future generations will benefit from the wisdom of the ancestors. Like Nwapa, Sutherland emphasizes women's foremost role in passing on cultural values; moreover, she also sees women as actively revitalizing the static traditions and working toward a more integrated modern African society. My discussion centers on Sutherland's play, *Foriwa*, and is supported by a few references to her retelling of an Ananse folk tale, *The Marriage of*

*Anansewa*; I examine Sutherland's use of drama as oraliterature, women's role in reviving the traditions, and the integration of two aspects of the oral tradition—the retelling of an African folk tale and the presentation of a traditional festival—as a way to resolve cultural conflict in modern African life. *Foriwa* as performance is pedagogical art: it presents the union of traditional values and modern technology through the collective process of the African community. Through the dramatic medium, Sutherland ensures that the traditions are passed on to the children, both rural and urban; furthermore, her vision of women as the moving force in revitalizing disintegrating rural communities illustrates how she has accepted and challenged the role designated to the African woman—not merely to reflect but expanding it to reform the orature of her foremothers. In this way, Sutherland has designed an Afrocentric "development plan" through artistic invention and the oral tradition, which emphasizes generational continuity and collective decision making.

Sutherland is well known as one of Ghana's most active voices in using traditional modes of theatre to promote social change. She has been instrumental in fostering indigenous drama in both her theatre groups and her plays. In 1958, she founded the Experimental Theatre Players, which became the Ghana Drama Studio in 1960. She also organized the "Kusum" group which performs plays and improvisations in English and local languages. Sutherland writes plays for children as well as for adults, and her impact has been felt through her children's plays and productions. Her goal has been to acknowledge traditional oral drama performed in villages, stimulate modern dramatic activities, and set up community theatres in rural areas. Her plays have been integral to her concept of theatre as a means of revitalizing rural life in African communities, and her best-known works, *Edufa* (1967), *Foriwa* (1967), and *The Marriage of Anansewa* (1975), all attempt to reconcile the conflict of Western and African cultural values in modern-day African society. Sutherland has taken her drama back to the village communities it came from, and her open-air theatres for dramatic performances and storytelling reflect her commitment to serve the community and educate future generations through the patterns and traditions of her ancestors.

Unlike the novel, which is a Western genre and undergoes great changes in an African woman's context such as Nwapa's, drama is integral to the historicity of African orature. In Kofi Awoonor's comprehensive *The Breast of the Earth*, he explains the full range of oral drama: "Drama includes masquerades, festivals, ritual performances and ceremonies pertaining to the secret societies. . . ; [even] the structure of the African folktale reveals an intense dramatic form" (69). It is unfortunate that Awoonor does not include any references to women's role in the oral tradition, therefore slighting the importance of orature in terms of child socialization. Nor does he mention either of his fellow Ghanaians, Sutherland or Aidoo, even though they both incorporate the orature in their works. Joel Adedeji, in "Theatre and Ideology in Africa," connects this traditional art form with emerging African nations' demands for national identity and decolonization. He sees the role of modern African theatre as fulfilling a cultural need on a national level that oral literature has done in local communities: "The theatre which is emerging . . . defines cultural values and consciously aspires towards an affirmation yet to be determined by the African peoples themselves" (79). Sutherland, as playwright and producer, creates plays of community affirmation; furthermore, she explores a broader definition of these cultural values by disclosing women's role in defining them.

Although, in her interviews, Sutherland refers in general to the rural communities who have been the keepers of the traditions and makes no explicit references to women's specific role in passing on the cultural values of her society, her plays attest to the predominant role that women have had. I am not suggesting that it is women alone who have maintained the traditions, merely that women's unique role has not been fully explored by oral historians. The play *Foriwa* illustrates women's function in the community; Sutherland's emphasis on writing and producing plays for children as well as for adults underscores her position as a woman deeply concerned with imparting the traditions of her ancestors to the children. She has also set up a model community environment—the "Kodzidan" experiment ("House of Stories"; Kodzi is one form of Akan folk tale) in Atwia-Ekumfi village (1964)—to create updated traditional African modes of drama for adults and children.[1] Poet Kofi Anyidoho, who has worked with Sutherland in a few of her projects, commented to me about the importance of Sutherland's programs for children: "I hadn't dreamed of writing for children, but we went on a research trip documenting the life of children in Ghana [which produced] a harvest of plays for children" (14 November 1982). Since the early 1950s, Sutherland has been promoting the writing, recording, and performing of works for children. Her concern is for the children who will pass on both the traditional culture and the cultural conflicts of modern Africa. Her fear has been that the clash of European and African cultures may break the continuum; her aspirations "for society to mind its cultural heritage" are reflected in her statement that "the traditional communities . . . have done a wonderful thing for the country: They have minded the culture. . . . [If] you have a work of drama, take it out to the village community; that is where your critics are!" (Nichols, *African Writers at the Microphone*, 107; 170).

Sutherland does not see dramatic works as taking the place of the oral tradition, but rather as part of a process in which the values and culture of her people are to be transmitted to the children of the following generations. In her modern productions, Sutherland has tried to capture the essence of the traditional modes of oral perform- ance, while also promoting the storytelling that goes on at home. Sutherland states in her introduction to *The Marriage of Anansewa* that although "storytelling is usually a domestic activity, there are in existence some specialist groups who have given it a full theatrical expression with established conventions. It is this system of tradi- tional theatre which I have developed" (v). Sutherland's ora- literature expands on the tales told in village compounds and the dramas performed in village squares by bringing to her plays this "formidable frame of reference derived from [the people's] con- sciousness of that dramatic heritage" (Adedeji 76).

As with oral performances, dramatic production is an excellent medium for communicating with the majority of Ghanaians for a number of reasons. First, the gap between orature and drama is discernibly less than that between orature and an alien form such as the novel. As Awoonor notes, all types of orature have dramatic elements in them. African drama is firmly rooted in the oral tradition and the collective retelling of moral tales within the framework of village life. Second, drama, as a medium for both entertainment and education, has advantages over other literary forms, since a play is performed and thereby does not isolate the nonliterate members of the community. The social issues and cultural representations in the plays are for the entire community; therefore, the emphasis must be on some type of oral transmission, as it has been in generations past. Moreover, a play can be easily adapted to the local language of a community. A play performed in English (or any other colonial language) will have a certain audience; a play enacted in the language of a community will have a broader audience. *Foriwa*, which was originally written in English, has been produced in Akan, and the possibility exists for its adaptation into many other African languages.

A third important aspect of the dramatic medium in an African context, particularly germane to this study, is the collective nature of the dramatic process. African drama is based on a close relationship between players and audience; the movement of the play forms an intricate bond between them, creating a community within the context of the performance. Although *The Marriage of Anansewa*, for example, makes use of the audience as a "crowd" or chorus—a direct adaptation of the structure of village story dramas—*Foriwa* involves the audience in another way: they become "integrated participants" in the play (July 60). In the stage directions to *Foriwa*, Sutherland states: "This play was intended to be performed in the open air in a street in any of the many small towns in Ghana." Since the play explores the moral erosion of small rural towns and villages, it is to be performed in that setting. In this way, the audience will address the conflict of the play immediately. It is a problem with which they are well acquainted; therefore, they will respond actively to the issues presented in the play. The collective sense of community which arises from the response of the audience to the players reflects the nature of communal decision making; moreover, the process by which the characters *as a collective whole* work to revitalize the community by reworking the traditions gives utterance to an African/feminist discourse.

In a discussion of the role of the African woman writer, Charlotte Bruner makes a statement concerning works of fiction, which equally applies to Sutherland's play: "The genre as tale, story or legend is an old form, containing perhaps a new message" (29). In addition to the collective quality of her work, Sutherland's retelling of an African folk tale is representative of African women's fiction. In light of the debt to the orature of the traditional culture, Sutherland's transformation of this tale has led some critics to see the play as "a simple moral tale, perhaps almost didactic in some ways, but not restricted by its morality or didacticism in any way"

(Banham and Wake 53). This rather off-handed compliment implies that the play is good in spite of its didactic nature, but that as a play based on the fundamentals of the oral tradition, its very didacticism fulfills its role as a tool to pass on and modify the cultural values of the society. The folk tale on which the structure of *Foriwa* is based is the same tale discussed in chapter 1—the tale of a beautiful but proud girl who refuses to marry any young man chosen by her family but decides instead to marry a handsome stranger. Yet in this play the choice of a stranger brings a "new life" rather than devastation, transforming the message of the old tale.

The play *Foriwa* is a later version of a short, allegorical tale Sutherland wrote, called "New Life in Kyerefaso" (1960). Both pieces are based on the transformation of this African tale used by mothers to warn their daughters away from unknown, handsome men. In the traditional form of the tale, whether the man turns into a python, a spirit, or a skull, the moral taught is that young women who disobey their families and don't listen to the wisdom of their elders will eventually meet disaster. As noted in the discussion about *Efuru*, this tale is very familiar to the young girls in villages across West Africa, and its meaning reflects the important role families have in marriage choices. Although Efuru's plight is sympathetically rendered by Nwapa, clearly the prophecy of the folk tale comes true for Efuru—she chooses both her husbands, and the marriages end in disaster! In *Foriwa*, however, Sutherland alters the meaning of this old tale to illustrate a different dilemma—how to build a nation out of the different ethnic groups in Ghana.

In both the story and the play, Foriwa, a beautiful, articulate school teacher, has returned home to celebrate the "New Life" festival with her town and her mother, the Queen Mother of Kyerefaso. Like her mother, Foriwa is disappointed by the general apathy of the town. She tells her mother in despair, "Everyone is waiting for someone from somewhere to come and do this or that for Kyerefaso. Who, and from where?" (8). The people of Kyerefaso are not as interested in responding to Foriwa's questions as they are in when she will finally accept a suitor and get married. Foriwa has many suitors, some very wealthy, but like the girl in the folk tale, she is not interested in any of them. In the earlier short story, Foriwa's displeasure with her suitors is circulated around the town, and "that evening there was heard a new song in the village" (114). The villagers use the well-known folk tale to warn Foriwa of the possible repercussions of her proud behavior, and although the song does not refer specifically to Foriwa, everyone in the town knows who the "maid" is. The song is sung to the maid and tells of a beautiful woman who would not marry Kwesi or Kwaw, but instead finds the man herself: "Her man looked like a chief, / Most splendid to see, / But he turned into a python, / He turned into a python, / And swallowed her up" ("New Life" 114).

The use of the oral tradition is apparent here in several ways. First, the community uses the folk tale to try to "educate" Foriwa. Since her own mother and mother's family seem unable to control Foriwa, the community will take on its role to help her conform. Second, within an oral context, songs are formulated to pass judgment on a present situation, emphasizing their importance in eliciting proper behavior. Finally, as Awoonor and others have noted, the orature always has a dramatic component: here the tale becomes a performed song.

Foriwa's identification with the folk tale breaks down when we look at each of the young women's motives. Unlike the proud girl, Foriwa has refused suitors not because of pride in her own beauty or disrespect for her family, but rather from a desire to help improve Kyerefaso and to find the man who will work with her. In *The Marriage of Anansewa*, a dramatic reworking of an Ananse tale, the grandmother tells her granddaughter Anansewa that there are other important qualities a man should have besides wealth:

> My grandchild, Anansewa, your old lady knows something about what is of real value in this world. You noticed that this outstretched hand of mine is empty, it contains nothing. And yet, this same empty hand will succeed in placing a gift into your brass bowl. What this hand is offering is this prayer of mine. May the man who comes to take you from our hands to his home be, above all things, a person with respect for the life of his fellow human beings. . . . (41–42)

In *Foriwa*, as in *The Marriage of Anansewa*, what is of real value is not necessarily material. The grandmother gives Anansewa advice in the form of a riddle, an aspect of the oral tradition. Moreover, her values come from the traditional culture before its distortion, in the present generation, by Western materialistic values, illustrated by the trickery of her son, Ananse. So when the Queen Mother asks Foriwa why she wants to refuse the present suitor, a man who "has salvaged his life from this decrepitude" by making a great success of his life materially, Foriwa answers that she will not join her life to a man who is interested merely in personal gain. She shudders at the kind of society he represents by ameliorating his own life at the expense of the community. She responds instead by approaching the subject of the town's deterioration and the Queen Mother's fights with the elders who care more for the words of the traditions than for what those words convey.

Foriwa is determined not to marry until she has helped rebuild the town and until both she and her mother agree on a man who has "respect for the life of his fellow human beings." Unlike the stranger in the tale—who is an evil, supernatural being—the stranger in this case is Labaran, an educated, socially active young man who is a Hausa from the north of Ghana. Labaran, a university graduate, is dismayed by the life offered to him in the capital, and he wanders through the countryside hoping to find his place in society. He ends up in Kyerefaso and remains there to try to understand the changes in his country: "Anyone who thinks I have nothing to do deceives himself. Because he sees no office? This is my office, this street; the people who use it are my work and education" (1). Labaran is derisively called "the son of an unknown tribe" by Sintim, one of the elders (19), and both his education and his commitment are held suspect by the Akan people of Kyerefaso. When the postmaster, who is working with Labaran to start a bookstore and reopen the school, asks Sintim to request the land from the Queen Mother, Sintim flatly refuses to be an "emissary for an Itani" (a disparaging term for someone from northern Ghana). The postmaster responds, "That's unfair. If this young man were a townsman, we could claim to be in possession of a *man of real value*" (18; emphasis added). Finally, it is Foriwa who secures the land for the bookstore.

The friendship and ensuing love relationship between Labaran and Foriwa turn the folk tale around, since their relationship does not presage disaster but the revitalization of the town of Kyerefaso. Moreover, the acceptance of Labaran by the Queen Mother and the town brings a new meaning to the tale: the stranger may not always be a villain, not when he is from your own country. The Queen Mother, who brings her community together, welcomes Labaran as future son-in-law and son of the soil as she states, "They say that we see with our eyes. That is true. But we are not often able to say that we see with our hearts also. . . . I have come to thank you for making your home on this foundation" (65). Rather than perceiving Sutherland's reworking of the tale as a breakdown of the traditions, we can envision the moral of the tale as an even stronger reflection of the community's values and the community's health: The initial tale still represents the importance of the alliance of families in choosing a mate, but the tale is also broadened to express another alliance—that of all the people of Ghana.

In her attention to the orature, Sutherland places herself in the traditional role of the African woman, "minding the culture" as she calls it, making sure that what is meaningful in the traditional life is maintained. But, as her altering of this folk tale suggests, she moves beyond the mere recording of past traditions; she helps to bring new life into the traditions and rituals which have become as stale as the old men in the play. Her aim, as woman and writer, is to alter certain traditions rather than disrupt them so as to communicate the cultural values of precolonial Africa with renewed meaning. In the article "The Atwia-Ekumfi Kodzidan—An Experimental African Theatre," E. Ofori Okyea praises Sutherland for helping revitalize that village with her model traditional theatre project:

> The KODZIDAN in Atwia has had some effects on the life of the village generally. There is, for instance, a cooperative store started in the village as a result of the performances done in other villages and from filming fees. A new block of buildings is being added to the school to make it more presentable. Atwia has become the 'eye' of villages around and *a few of the young men in Accra have returned to inject some new life into the village.* (83; emphasis added)

Clearly, Atwia is the realized project that led Sutherland to rework her story "New Life in Kyerefaso" into the play *Foriwa*, but Okyea seems to have missed an important aspect of the revitalization—the role of women. Okyea does not mention that the leader of Atwia was a woman, "Lady Chief Nana Okoampa" (Crane 490). More-over, it is plausible to think that some of the young *women* from Accra have also joined hands to work in Atwia, but the writer has chosen, as usual, to mention only the young men. This misrepresentation of history (herstory) is typical of the neglect women as a group have suffered from historians, anthropologists, and politicians in terms of the role they have played in the past.[2] The point is particularly relevant here because, in this play, it is precisely the young woman Foriwa who returns to Kyerefaso to "inject some new life in the village." Sutherland, in her choice of characters, emphasizes the role women play in the process of decolonization and the revitalization of communities through traditional customs and values. The position of Queen Mother and the return of Foriwa, as well as the relationship between mother and daughter, exemplify Sutherland's intention to document women's unique contribution to the continuation of the traditional culture.

Although she is helped by her daughter Foriwa and the "stranger" Labaran, the Queen Mother is the moving force in the revitalization of the town of Kyerefaso. She brings her community together through a new interpretation of the traditional customs. It is the Queen Mother's duty as "mother" to nurture her community and insure that the values are maintained. In "Asante Queen Mothers in Government and Politics in the Nineteenth Century," Agnes Akosua Aidoo comments, "Like all Akan women, the Queen Mother derived her position from the matrilineal social organization. The Akan trace descent through the female line. The woman is the genetically significant link between successive generations" (65). As indicated earlier, the woman is also the valuational link between generations, so the role of Queen Mother is understood to include her ability to keep the culture's values alive. From precolonial times, the Queen Mother has been the authority in her village, working with the elders of the village to govern the community. As the "Ohemma" (the foremost authority on the genealogy of the royal matrilineage), the Queen Mother was considered "the custodian of the 'custom' " (Arhin 92–94). The power and authority of the Queen Mother and the Ohemma—the most important female leader of the clan—was far greater in precolonial Africa, but the Queen Mother has remained a prominent figure in modern Ghana.[3]

In *Foriwa*, the conflict between the Queen Mother and Sintim, the elder most resistant to change, on her right as a woman to hold the position of authority does not, as some critics have suggested, arise from the unusual circumstances of having a woman in control; rather, it stems from the colonialist disruption of a traditional practice. When the Queen Mother attempts to revitalize the "path-clearing" ceremony, Sintim expresses his disgust at this woman acting as leader:

> I am going to sprinkle ritual food all over Kyerefaso, I Sintim, Son
> of the stalwart Odum tree. . . . I shall not stand by and see the town

disgraced. How when there are cocks here, should a hen be allowed to strut around in this manner, without getting her head pecked? (38).

Sintim represents the seemingly universal disdain for women that men have, but he also reflects a colonialist view that women have no place in positions of authority.[4] The issue is not that women were of equal status to men in precolonial Black Africa, but that their role in the political sphere was respected whether they governed only the female population or the whole society. The determination that women display in responding to the conflicts in the play—the Queen Mother's opposition to the elders and the staleness of the traditions, Foriwa's desire to return home to help improve the community rather than marry a rich man—does not necessarily arise from notions of modern feminism but stem from a traditional view of a woman's place in society as wife, mother, *and* active member/leader of the community.

The Queen Mother, tired of the apathy of her town, decides to try to arouse the community by revitalizing an upcoming festival. Her aim is to demonstrate how far the society has strayed from the original spirit of the ceremony. The inability of the elders to adapt the values of the past to present experience disheartens her and makes her wonder why she does not go somewhere she can breathe—"somewhere perhaps where, like a living tree, I can shed my wasted leaves to grow new ones, and flowers, and fruit. . . ." Yet when Foriwa asks her why she doesn't leave, she answers, "I'm rooted here. I agreed to be mounted like a gorgeous sacrifice to tradition" (8). Although the Queen Mother speaks negatively of being mounted like a sacrifice in her moment of distress, her appreciation of her roots gives her the strength to reformulate the traditions to breathe new life into her town. Sutherland's use of the tree of life imagery (from the roots to the fruit on the branches) adds to the perception of generational continuity in this play. The Queen relates her own place in the society with that of this shrine tree; she is rooted to her community, tied to the past, but she also hopes to breathe life into the town so it will bear fruit. Moreover, in her plan to revivify the festival, she describes the custom as the fruit that has matured from the seeds of the ancients through the nurturing of each generation: "For a long time I've been trying to find a way to

make the people of Kyerefaso see; to see at least that for our ancestors, custom was the fruit they picked from the living branches of
life" (25). The Queen's title as mother of the community and the
references to the rebirth of the traditions in modern form illustrate
how women bring to bear their role as mothers to include nurturing
of the land and the traditions of its people.

In *The Black Woman Cross-Culturally*, Filomina Steady emphasizes that, for the Black woman, being a child-bearer is not necessarily a restrictive role but is one tied to land fertility and the oral
tradition: "Women's roles as child-bearers and food producers are
often associated with fertility of the land, and this is implicit in much
of the ritual. This life-giving quality endows women not only with
much prestige but equates them with the life-giving force itself"
(29–30). In the first chapter, we witnessed Efuru's finding another
way in which to fulfill her role in society; in the case of the Queen
Mother, the role of the African woman is expanded to a nurturer of
those she governs, and her responsibilities as the educator of her
children extend to the entire community. It is her function to bring
the family (community) together to maintain the traditions for the
generations to come.

Foriwa has many of the same characteristics as her mother which
enable her to accept the challenge of rebuilding the decaying town
of Kyerefaso. Like her mother, she is independent and believes in
her own opinions, but she also feels deeply for the community in
which she was born and wants to be part of its rebirth. Her despair
arises from the failure of the town to work out some compromise
between the traditional values of the ancestors and the technological
changes of modern Africa. The town's apathy brings on a restless-
ness in her (8), but like the Atwia youths in Accra, she hopes, by
remaining, to "inject some new life" in her community. It may
appear cursorily that Foriwa disregards tradition by not marrying her
rich suitor and choosing to stay in Kyerefaso instead of making a
better life for herself in Accra; however, one can argue that Foriwa is
responding to the earlier traditions and values of her culture, before
Christian/Western doctrine categorized woman as "helpmate"
rather than a citizen in her own right. Maryse Condé comments:
"African women stand at the very heart of the turmoil of the continent. Going back to colonialism, one is tempted to say that they
were the principal victims of the encounter with the West. The

missionaries did not understand the position they held in their families and societies" (133). Therefore, with a disruption of the culture
as violent as that of colonialism, a strike against the atrophied traditions of a town might actually be closer at heart to the original
cultural values than adherence to those distorted traditions. For this
reason, Foriwa rejects an easy solution for her individual life and
remains at home as part of a communal effort to bring new life to
Kyerefaso. Tired of being a "runaway daughter" (35), she chooses
to remain unmarried until she has fulfilled another role of the
precolonial African woman, her responsibility to her community.

Foriwa's decision to stay in Kyerefaso is tied to her mother's
reforming of the path-clearing festival. The conflict between the
Queen Mother's desire for what is best for her daughter and
Foriwa's answer to her mother's call is a germane example of how
this play focuses on the reinterpretation of traditional culture. In
spite of her mother's protests, Foriwa answers her mother's call (as
Queen Mother) for *all* of the children of Kyerefaso to return and
help rebuild the town. During the ceremony, Foriwa declares her
intentions to the town: "When the Linguist tells this story, he shall
also say that I, your own daughter answered to your call" (53). And
after the festival, she expresses her relief at finally making a commitment: "Mother, I have solved the conflict in myself. Your words
down there today threw me up like a bird, and I have found my way
home again." Her mother answers her with distress: "Oh, my child,
why couldn't you have waited for some sign of promise in this place
before you spoke. . . . I should praise you for it, *were I only Queen
Mother and not your mother also*" (55; emphasis added). Foriwa
does not accept her mother's advice to satisfy her own individual
desires. Instead, she listens to her mother in a much deeper way: she
responds to the words spoken by the mother of the community, the
mother with the wisdom handed down to her through the ancestors. As Foriwa's mother and as leader of the community, the Queen
Mother has passed on the values of her culture to her daughter so
that Foriwa could not respond in any other way. Thus, the play
portrays women not only as maintaining the customs, but as actively
altering and reinterpreting these customs to make them applicable
for modern Ghanaian life. Sutherland has documented women's
important role in keeping custom ripe and alive for the next generations to pick.

The climax of the play is the revitalization of an important traditional festival. The Queen Mother has chosen to revivify the annual "path-clearing" festival, a ceremony of new life. She decides to conduct a mock ceremony the evening before the festival to point out how far the town has strayed from the original meaning of the ceremony. The ritual glorifies the hard work that went into the founding of Kyerefaso and celebrates the beginning of the town. The mock festival is the turning point in the play because the community, and in a sense the audience, too, must choose whether to work for that new life or leave the ceremony as an empty ritual. This scene illustrates a dialectic between the action in the play and the aims of the playwright. Festivals have been seen as a major influence on contemporary African playwrights (Asagba 88), and here Sutherland recreates the festival scene in the play while also using this form of folk drama as her source.

The Queen Mother asks the people of the town to come *as if* to the festival. This causes much confusion in the town, but the participants come. The Linguist, the oral historian of the town, explains, "We made her Queen because we love her; beyond the right of inheritance. . ." (43). When everyone is assembled, the Queen Mother lets them go through the ceremony as they do each year, but she stops them in the middle of the ritual. She asks the community when they will live up to the words of the ceremony. Foriwa, who stands beside her mother, refuses to dance in the ceremony because she cannot find anyone "with whom this new life shall be built." The Queen Mother, empowered by the truth of her daughter's statement, expresses her own feelings to the group:

> Sitting here seeing Kyerefaso die, I am no longer able to bear the mockery of the fine, brave words of this ceremony of our festival. . . . No, we have turned Kyerefaso into a death bed from which our young people run away to seek elsewhere, the promise of life we've failed to give them here. (51)

The belief in the continuity of a culture from the ancestors to the descendants is a major aspect of traditional African society, and that belief is integrally related to the land; if the next generation leaves the land "to seek elsewhere, the promise of life," then the lineage will be broken and the fiber of the society destroyed. The Queen Mother realizes that the disintegration of her community is inevitable if the children leave and do not make a commitment to their culture. Through the shock of disrupting the ritual, she attempts to incite the people of Kyerefaso to work toward creating a viable alternative to the city and its Western materialism. Each of Sutherland's three plays deals with the conflict of Western and traditional values, specifically individual wealth in opposition to community responsibility. In *Edufa*, the result is tragic for the protagonists: Edufa's wife Ampona dies as a consequence of his desire for material gain; the treatment of this theme is comic in *The Marriage of Anansewa*, although the message is the same. *Foriwa* goes one step beyond the critique and tries to create a performance atmosphere which reconciles these conflicting values in contemporary African life through a woman-centered perspective. In the play, the educated individual is no more or less necessary to the revitalization of the town than the workers or dancers, and the Queen Mother's admonishment to the Scholar's Union for calling the *Asafo* dancers "illiterate" clearly reflects this position (47).

The Queen Mother's reforming of the mock ceremony to awaken Kyerefaso to the real meaning of the festival reflects Sutherland's aim to arouse the audience to use their traditions to revitalize their own communities. The reconciliation of the Queen Mother and the elders, particularly the abrasive Sintim, her acceptance of Labaran into the community and her own home, and Foriwa's decision to remain in Kyerefaso all illustrate a positive step toward the revival of rural communities and the unity of all the people of Ghana. The structure of the play reflects this collective, nonhierarchical (female) tradition in that there is no hero and no villain to either save or destroy, but all work together to improve the town's condition. The revitalization of Kyerefaso is shared between the main protagonists—the Queen Mother, Foriwa, Labaran, and the postmaster—and it is their cooperation with the elders and the townsfolk which brings the town to life. Dialectically, however, it is the Queen Mother, as nurturer of the town and custodian of the custom, who motivates the community through the transformation of the oral traditions. Although a "monarch," she compels the society to face its problems not by authorial force but by transforming a ceremony in which all participate. She tells her intentions to the community through the Linguist: "I knew of no way of reaching my people better with such thoughts than to use this ceremony of our festival as my interpreter" (51). In this way, the Queen Mother is passing on the customs of the ancestors to future generations, not as archaic remnants of a time past, but as part of a living tradition which keeps the culture itself alive. And her manner of renewing the rituals is in accordance with the way women have been passing on the values of their cultures, by repetition and alteration, throughout generations. For as feminist critic Jane Marcus says, it is the transformation, rather than the permanence of the creation, which is at the heart of most women's art.[5]

Although her challenge to the community is the main motivating force in revitalizing Kyerefaso, the Queen Mother's ability to pass on those values and motivations to her daughter is equally important. As we will also see in Paule Marshall's *Praisesong*, it is often the daughters who take the challenge to their own generation. When Foriwa declines to dance in the mock ceremony because she does not find the young man with whom this new life could be built, she is actively taking up her mother's challenge and altering the ritual on her own. She tells the crowd, "He is not here, mother. I don't see him in these empty eyes. I see nothing alive here, mother, nothing alive" (50). Foriwa's declaration here is important for two reasons. First, Foriwa emphasizes her mother's statement that until the community words "'I love my land' [cease] to be the empty croaking of a vulture on the rubbish heap" (50), the festival and the traditions will mean nothing. Second, Foriwa finds "the young man" in Labaran, the stranger not included in the festival but instrumental in the revitalization process; therefore, her comments foreshadow the time when all those who share the values of the society and want to work to improve it will be welcomed. Labaran, as one of the young men, must join the young women to build this new life, blending traditional values and modern experience. The acceptance of Labaran as Foriwa's husband-to-be presages the unity of Ghana's different ethnic groups, altering the folk tale; yet, the original meaning of the tale also stands. Foriwa has chosen her own husband, but the marriage will be consecrated only with the Queen Mother's approval and by the traditions of her own culture. Both Foriwa's involvement in the reforming of the festival and Labaran's acknowledgment that their marriage will have to wait until their actions have proved true to the words spoken in the ceremony illustrate a nonsexist partnership in which the men and women of the community work together to improve their lives. Even Sintim, the antifeminist, responds to the power of both the Queen Mother and Foriwa; he comments that Foriwa has "the fire of those courageous women who made men of our ancestors" (61). Of course, he is able to see women's strength only in terms of what they do for men, but he plainly states that Foriwa's strength has been passed down to her through her foremothers.

One final comment on the use of modern technology in the play to promote the oral tradition may be helpful here. After the challenge is taken up by the performers in the mock ceremony, the word is passed from compound to compound that the community will be prepared for both the festival the next day and the Queen's invocation that they breathe new life into Kyerefaso. As the people disperse, the sound of the Queen's voice is heard once again from the foundation, challenging Kyerefaso to bring meaning and life to the words of the traditions. But the Queen is not repeating herself; it is Labaran who has taped the Queen's voice with his "recording machine" (56). Again, in the final scene, Labaran plays the tape of Foriwa's speech as the others look on, recording this moment for posterity (64). The tape recorder documents the community's history in a more precise though less creative manner than the words of the orators, and it has a place in the society in terms of passing down the *exact* words of a speech or story. The recorder, as handled by Labaran, exemplifies a modern convenience utilized to enhance the orature. Yet, in spite of its precision, neither the tape recorder nor the man who uses it can take the place of the orature and the women who tell the tales to their children in every home, every compound. The art of the oral tradition depends upon the teller of the tale as well as the tale itself--whether it be a "master" teller or undocumented village women storytellers. Sutherland does not see literary drama taking the place of oral drama in the community, nor, one hopes, will the tape recorder replace the orature of the traditional culture, passed on through generations.

In her three published plays for adults, Sutherland's aim has been to focus on the kind of values that are being passed on to the children—what will become of traditional culture, weakened by colonial/neocolonial domination, if the present generation does not maintain their oral traditions and reform them to fit modern Ghanaian society. As performance oraliterature, *Foriwa* works toward a resolution of cultural conflicts by its use in the revitalization of rural communities. Sutherland's emphasis on women's role in "minding the culture" and bringing new life into the old traditions mirrors her concern for and active participation in strengthening the bonds between the African past and future generations. Her performances and productions, her village education for children, and her plays themselves illustrate a playwright tied not only to the traditions and customs of the African continuum but also secure in her own place as an African woman passing on the values of her foremothers to the children.

# 3

## Ama Ata Aidoo,
### *The Dilemma of a Ghost*

If you educate a man, you educate an individual. If you educate a woman, you educate a nation.[1]

Kwegyir Aggrey

■ Ama Ata Aidoo, like her sister Ghanaian Efua Sutherland, has been extremely active in promoting her culture's traditions through her writing and productions, and her post as Ghana's Minister of Culture and Education. She is one of Africa's most outspoken writers, especially in regard to the position of women, and is author to literary works in all genres: poetry, short stories, plays, and a novel, *Our Sister Killjoy* (1979). All of Aidoo's work conveys her social vision, her commitment to write oraliterature, and her belief in reworking the traditions to create a more integrated African society; but unlike Sutherland's soft touch, her criticisms of the unfair use of traditional values and imported Western culture are extremely harsh. Her outspokenness toward male dominance in African countries has earned her a rather antagonistic response from some male critics; her writings aim toward the betterment of women's position as well as a global concern for the liberation of Black peoples everywhere. Aidoo's social vision includes all the children of the African diaspora; her position as storyteller and cultural advisor is expanded to the acceptance and understanding of all the descendants of Africa. In this last chapter in the African section, my discussion extends beyond the examination of women-specific retention of African cultural values to include the conflicts and continuity of those of African descent throughout the diaspora. To this end, I examine Aidoo's first published play, *The Dilemma of a Ghost* (1965), including pertinent references to a later play, *Anowa* (1970), and her novel. I focus on Aidoo's debt to the orature of her foremothers, the role of the two community women as narrators, generational continuity in the African kinswomen, and the problems of the reunion of those of the diaspora illustrated by the antagonism toward and later compassion for the lost daughter of the diaspora, the African-American Eulalie.

Aidoo was very young (twenty-two) when she wrote *The Dilemma of a Ghost*. Nonetheless, even then she saw the plight of the Black person in a global sense. In a mostly antagonistic interview by Nigerian critic Theo Vincent, Aidoo manages to express her views on the diaspora:

> I don't know how people react when they leave Africa and go to places outside where there are concentrations of other Black peoples, but for me it was incredible. I just couldn't believe that I could cross the whole of the Atlantic and go and find all of these people who are like people at home. . . . But definitely this is the reason I keep coming back to this because I think it is part of what is eating us up. You can't cover up history. . . . It is time we faced the question of what happened that so many of us are in Harlem and so many in the West Indies. . . . You see, grief accepted is grief overcome. (35)

In both plays examined, Aidoo tries to come to terms with the fact of the African diaspora. In *Anowa*, she explores African complicity in the slave trade. In *The Dilemma of a Ghost*, she looks at the repercussions of the slave trade on a personal level, the marriage of an African-American woman to a Ghanaian man. The story is a simple one: Ato Yawson, a Ghanaian studying in the United States, meets Eulalie Rush, another student, and they fall in love. After deciding that they will "wait" to have children, they marry and return to his home–Ato with his pumped up sense of himself and his Western education and Eulalie with her typical American misconceptions of Africa mixed with a real desire to finally "belong" somewhere. The major conflict of the play stems from Eulalie's inability to adapt to the society she has entered, Ato's family members' expectations of the returning "scholar," and Ato's total amnesia concerning the values and traditions of his culture.

In "The Image of the Afro-American in African Literature," Bernth Lindfors comments, "This is a drama not only of marital discord but of cultural conflict" (20). Indeed, but since the conflict is between two cultures with similar ancestry, the encounter takes on more significance than if Eulalie had been a white American. Precisely because Eulalie is a Black American, the play explores more than marital discord and cultural conflicts by examining what Aidoo feels has been covered up by a denial of history—Africa's relationship to its descendants in the Americas. And in this play as in the works of the other writers in this study, it is the women who work to reconcile what appears to be a conflict of cultures but what may in fact be a family quarrel.

Critical response to *Dilemma of a Ghost* has focused mainly on Ato's "dilemma" and Eulalie's disagreeableness, with some attention to Aidoo's language style and her use of the oral tradition. Unfortunately, the attention accorded to the "hero" Ato and, therefore, the anti-hero Eulalie in isolation has denied a holistic interpretation of the play. What is left out is the role of the women—Ato's mother, Esi Kom, the grandmother, Nana, and the two women storytellers—who structure and restructure the play and, for Esi Kom in particular, move toward reconciliation. So if Aidoo has chosen to write a play not merely about a young man's "dilemma" but about a group of women, their conflicts, their capacity for understanding and education, a critic may ignore them to find a hero of *his* own. For although Ato is integral to the story, his actions hardly make him a hero, and he is no more the main protagonist than either Esi Kom or Eulalie. I make this crucial point because I hope to examine this play in light of the position of the women, the Africans who have been reduced to silence, and the Black American whose character has been distorted by the overemphasis on the African man's point of view. It is through a community of characters that the open moral of the dilemma tale works. Like the other African women writers discussed here, Aidoo uses her skill as a storyteller to create modern folk art as performance oraliterature. The play is a dilemma tale, not only the dilemma of the "been-to" but more importantly the dilemma of the Africans in facing the history which has made a diaspora and the dilemma of these women of how to pass down the values of the culture to the child of African descent.

In the first two chapters in the African section, I focused on the writers' debt to the orature of their foremothers; Aidoo is no exception. In her short stories and plays, Aidoo has expanded the role of the domestic storyteller by utilizing her culture's orature in the structure of her writings; moreover, she emphasizes the way in which women pass on and maintain, defend, and sometimes confront the traditional values and customs of their society. Aidoo is committed to a total vision of African women's history and herstory as she states in "Unwelcome Pals and Decorative Slaves":

> Unless a particular writer commits his or her energies, actively, to exposing the sexist tragedy of women's history; protesting the on-going degradation of women; celebrating their physical and intellectual capabilities, and above all, unfolding a revolutionary vision of the role of women tomorrow, as dreamers thinkers and doers; they cannot be described as feminist writers. . . .
>
> In the meantime, women are half of humanity. *Our lives too are simple songs that can be sung simply and ordinary tales that can be told ordinarily.* (32; 33; emphasis added)

Aidoo's discourse is part of this revolutionary struggle because she envisions a role for women that blends traditional culture with a global perspective; through the ordinary tales and simple songs, there may be a way of bridging gaps, reconciliation. Aidoo sees her work as not only reflecting her culture and society but reforming it, and since she understands that it is the orature which has done this in the past, she, like Sutherland, structures her drama on this vibrant art:

> I think any discussion of African drama has to start with the so-called oral traditions, because if African theatre is really going to gain any strength, some of it has to come from there. Everybody needs a backbone. If we do not refer to the old traditions, it is almost like operating with amnesia. You wake up one morning, you can't remember yesterday, and you intend to go on today and plan for tomorrow. That worries me. (*Issue* 124)

Aidoo is clearly aware of the dialectical relationship of orature and literature—and emphasizes the connections between them. In her collection of short stories, *No Sweetness Here*, Aidoo attempts to write tales that can be told, recited to an audience. The short story, seen as an evolution of the tale, is envisioned by Aidoo as a partnership of these two forms, oral and written, and can be appreciated on both levels: "I believe that when a writer writes a short story, it should be possible for the writer to sit before an audience and tell them the story. . . . We don't always have to write for readers, we can write for listeners" (Lautré 24). Aidoo creates oraliterature, using her work as a politically functional tool to confront the conflicts of modern African society in the manner her ancestors faced the conflicts of their own generations. Her novel, *Our Sister Killjoy*, reflects further exploration into a blending of oral and written traditions by its extensive use of dialogue, song, and poetry, in addition to the communal, female perspective of "our sister." In all of her works, Aidoo's concern focuses on the position and plight of women because, as anthropologist Marion Kilson suggests about traditional African storytellers, there is a "relevance of the narrator's sex to characters in the tale, for invariably the protagonists of the tale include one with whom the narrator can identify" ("Women and African Literature," 163). Aidoo, as the authorial "narrator" of her works, reflects the tradition of women storytellers and cultural advisors and takes that role into the modern political and social arena.

In *Anowa* and *The Dilemma of a Ghost*, Aidoo actively incorporates the oral tradition by the retelling of an African folk tale in the first play and by the use of a dilemma tale as the structure for the second. Furthermore, since drama is a performed art, her plays are received by listeners as in oral dramas of village folk art. Commenting on the creation of *Anowa*, Aidoo states that the idea for the play came from a legend that she originally heard from her mother: "The original story, which in a way was in the form of a song . . . is more or less my own rendering of a kind of . . . legend, because, according to my mother, who told me the story, it is supposed to have happened" (Lautré 23). The transformation of a legend told by mother to daughter is a further example of the way in which tales are passed down through generations of women. Aidoo's reworking of this legend also evokes the folk tale discussed earlier—that of the beautiful young girl who picks her husband in opposition to her family's choices—and, in this case, the marriage ends in suicide for them both. The old woman storyteller, who recounts much of the story, exclaims: "That Anowa is something else! Like all the beautiful maidens in the tales, she has refused to marry any of the sturdy men who have asked for her hand in marriage. No one knows what is wrong with her" (9). Like Nwapa and Sutherland, Aidoo is captivated by this folk tale which has characterized such an important aspect of the African woman's life, and as a creative storyteller, she has turned the tale around to fit her own telling. Yet in some ways, her reworking of the folk tale is closer to the original tale than the others since Nwapa's version is solely an underpinning to the plot of the novel and Sutherland's version changes the ending. Aidoo's tale is by far the most tragic of the three and follows the lines of the folk tale completely. Yet, ironically, it is Aidoo who questions in a most overt manner the basic premise of the tale itself and what women's position in the society is to be.

Anowa, the main figure in the play, is not the proud, self-centered beauty of the folk tale; her apparent contrariness comes from a different source. She not only chooses her husband according to another set of values than her parents', she is also motivated by a higher moral order than those around her. She rebels against her mother's guidance in this instance, but as Ebele Eko notes, the rebellion is not against her as "mother" but as representative of "societal authority and expectation" (141). Later, the community is pleased, since she and her husband are successful traders. They become very wealthy because her husband turns their trade to that of human cargo, but she refuses any of the benefits from what she considers, and we know, to be the most devastating of occupations—the slave trade. Anowa is condemned for her stance rather than praised for it by her community; the greed of the people outweighs the good moral judgments encoded in the culture, and as in present times, the conventions are suited to fit the greed. Anowa, who is childless, at first feels that she has lost her right to children by her involvement in this inhuman occupation. As I noted in the chapter on *Efuru*, childlessness is rarely seen as an accident of nature. Finally, Anowa realizes that it is her husband, Kofi Ako, who has exhausted his "masculinity acquiring slaves and wealth" (61). The old woman storyteller ends the play by stating: "This is the type of happening out of which we get stories and legends" (63). As part of her modern interpretation of this legend and the African folk tale, Aidoo bears upon the oral tradition and women's role in it to question the values and history of her culture as well as explore the impact of their collective past on hers and future generations.

Maryse Condé, in an article on Nwapa and Aidoo, comments

that their works illustrate that "the African woman has an important role to play in the future of Africa and in the past it was the same. But for all this faith, there remains a doubt, a doubt on the value of their world nurtured by the daily sight of their complex and contradictory society torn between different ideals and poisoned by self-distrust" (143). Condé's point is well taken in terms of the gloom that surrounds the play *Anowa*, but it is unfortunate that she so quickly dismisses *The Dilemma of a Ghost* as a "flimsy comedy," since it is in this play, as well as in her later novel *Our Sister Killjoy*, that Aidoo's questioning of values and moral issues concerning traditional and modern African society is explored with a more positive and assured vision.

Although *The Dilemma of a Ghost* is more contemporary and less closely aligned to any one folk tale than *Anowa*, the structure of the play is deeply rooted in the orature. As I have mentioned and others have noted, the play itself is in the form of an African dilemma tale. Roger Abrahams refers to this type of folk tale in the introduction to *African Folktales*:

> [These dilemma tales are] often explored in conversations, especially among adults and children. . . . These African versions throw the floor open to debate, demonstrating yet again that in the African context the function of story telling is to initiate as much as to instruct. . . . Even when such a moral "last word" does arise, it commonly is at once so divisive and open-ended in its implications that it calls for further discussion. (16-17)

One major aspect of the dilemma tale is that the ending does not leave one with a strict or simple moral; the questions posed in the tale are left open for further discussion and thought. "Dilemma tales of [this] type, which are more often resolved by the narrator, involve moral and ethical judgement and are considerably more interesting because of the light they throw on cultural norms and values" (Bascom 14).

The questions concerning the culture's norms and values that Aidoo raises in *The Dilemma of a Ghost* are indeed difficult ones without easy solutions, and the issues are ones that confront modern-day Ghanaian society. But Aidoo's use of a dilemma tale to tell her story also reflects her position as a woman in the society: As cultural advisor and maintainer/reformer of traditions, Aidoo uses

the play to "initiate and instruct" the young on the conflicts of
modern African life and the diaspora (this play is taught and performed in secondary schools throughout West Africa). Furthermore,
the use of the dilemma tale to explore conflicts in modern life gives
the play a sense of structural continuity for its audience and insures
the growth of this traditional folk art.

Aidoo utilizes this oral art form in two ways in *The Dilemma of a
Ghost*. First, there is the obvious dilemma of Ato, the "been-to."
The title of the play is a reference to a children's folk tale/song
about a wretched ghost seen at a crossroads, wandering up and
down, wondering whether to go to Cape Coast or Elmina.[2] The
ghost seems immobilized and, rather than coming to any decision,
keeps repeating "I don't know, I can't tell" (23). Two children, a
girl and a boy who look just like Ato did at that age, sing the song
that awakens Ato. He runs on to the empty stage—the children have
disappeared—and he can't decide whether he actually heard the
song or was dreaming. In his confusion, Ato exclaims: "Damn this
ghost at the junction. . . . I used to wonder what the ghost was
doing there. . . . But why should I dream about all these things
now?" (24).

Ato's preoccupation with the ghost's dilemma mirrors his inability to come to terms with his own situation. He appears to be the
human representation of the ghost because he is unable to deal with
the dilemma in his life—how to reconcile his wife and Western
education to the traditions and cultural practices of his family. Like
the ghost, he manages mostly to say "I don't know, I can't say" in
his own way. For example, his family comes to see him because they
are concerned that, after over a year of marriage, there is no sign of
Eulalie's pregnancy. Since having children is integral to traditional
marriage, the family wonders what is wrong. But when they ask him,
he answers "nothing" rather than explaining to them that he and
Eulalie are using birth control (39–41). Ato does not confront the
problems in his life but is left in a quandary which he is incapable of
solving; hence, the dilemma of the ghost.

The second dilemma of the play is less overt and more difficult to
resolve: This dilemma is one that both the Africans and Eulalie, the
Black American, face in relationship to the diaspora and each other.
For Eulalie, the dilemma arises in her desire to finally "belong somewhere" where she is not treated as part of an oppressed minority

counterposed by her American upbringing and its prejudicial attitudes about Africa. Her conflicting emotions about Africa mirror the concerns examined in the second section of this study. For the Africans, their dilemma comes from an insistence to ignore a violently negative aspect of their past and, therefore, a conflict in how to relate to the daughter of African descent, a daughter of slaves. Aidoo speaks about this surprising lack of historicity in an oral tradition which spans centuries: "The oral traditions can tell you about the migrations that happened about a thousand years ago, and yet events that happened two to three hundred years ago are completely blanketed over" (Vincent 7). Aidoo's compulsion to address this subject which has been silenced in the culture is apparent; in *The Dilemma of a Ghost*, this theme holds great potential for dialogue and thought on the community and continental level. The play becomes a vehicle for more than an exploration of the marital/cultural conflict of Ato and Eulalie; it directs itself to a dilemma which has had deep repercussions for Africa and its diaspora.

As part of her creative aim to recount both the silenced past and the traditional culture, Aidoo has adapted English—a language of domination—to fit her tale. Although Aidoo is very insistent about English being a dead end as an African literary language, she has managed to cope with the conflict by injecting this colonial language with her own.[3] Her ability to capture the flavor of Akan within the construct of English sentences underscores her oraliterary style. Her forte is in reproducing the voices of rural Ghanaians, especially the women. In *The Dilemma of a Ghost*, the voice of the community, as well as the voice of the storyteller, always comes through the mouths of women. The language of Aidoo's African women, from the prelude's Bird of the Wayside to the two women narrators, from Esi Kom and Monka to Nana, is extremely poetic and lyrical, illustrating once again the domestic basis for much folk art and orature in African culture.

The conflict of the play is introduced to us in the prelude by the Bird of the Wayside, an "asthmatic old hag" (1). She is not a particularly attractive old woman, but she appears wise. She is perhaps an ancestor, but certainly an outsider, as her name implies. There are many reverberations in the play's imagery concerning the Bird of the Wayside—both Ato and Eulalie seem to be hanging their nest by the wayside (9)—but what is most relevant to this study is her role as storyteller. It is the old woman who sets the stage for this dilemma

tale. She speaks to the audience in verse, with a powerful, omniscient voice; she questions the audience in the style of these tales, on
the explanation of the bizarre happenings in the home of Ato's
family, the Odumna Clan: "I can furnish you with reasons why /
This and that and other things / Happened. But stranger, / What
would you have me say / About the Odumna Clan?" (1). She sets
up the cultural environment as well as the dilemma. This home,
which has been known throughout generations as revered, wealthy,
and full of children, has lost much in the making of the "One
Scholar," but what have they gained? She refuses to tell us what
happens but opens the play with her question.

The Bird of the Wayside remains in the play only during the
prelude, but within the main body of the play there are two other
women, called 1st Woman and 2nd Woman, who narrate this dilemma tale. With the use of tales within tales, proverbs and parables,
the two women pass on the tenets of the oral tradition as part of
their duty to future generations, and in this case, to the audience. In
the course of the play they act as neighbors, respond to the various
goings-on that they narrate, and express the community's opinion
on events and issues, even when they themselves may not agree with
it. Although in the prelude the Bird of the Wayside introduces Ato
and Eulalie (in America) to the audience, the two women open the
first act on Ghanaian soil. Unlike the isolation of Eulalie and Ato in
the prelude, the first act prepares us for a communal perspective on
the events to happen. Since the two women are participants in the
play as well as storytellers, they are involved with the actions of the
other characters and constantly muse over incidents as they tell us
the story. Their stance is usually apart from the main protagonists,
commenting on the action of the play while going to fetch water, to
farm, or to market. Aidoo's placement of the two village women in
the design of the play emphasizes their role as community voice. As
storytellers, they work as a framing device in most of the acts, and
when they appear in the middle of an act, it is usually at a traumatic
break. Their discussions open and close Act One, they open Act
Two and Act Four, and they play an important role at the climax of
Act Five. Interestingly, the beginning of Act Three does not begin
with any of the main protagonists either; the boy and girl open it
with their song. The song of the ghost's dilemma also ends the play,
leaving the audience to address the open-ended moral of this dilemma tale. With the use of the Bird of the Wayside, the two

women, and the children with their song, Aidoo is clearly structuring the play as a village tale. The multiple narrators are constantly commenting, judging, and questioning as part of their relationship with the audience, who is being enticed to do the same.

Act One opens with the two women returning home from fetching water at the riverside. Their first discussion illustrates a major issue in the play as well as one which is of great significance to the African woman—children and childlessness. In *Efuru*, we saw that childlessness was the main conflict of the novel; in this play, it appears to be a secondary concern but is actually a major motif. Their discussion on the merits of children/childlessness exposes the subordinate status of women in the village as well as introduces the plight of Esi Kom and her son Ato to the audience. The two women, as I noted earlier, speak in a versified English:

> *1st Woman*: Ah! And yet I thought I was alone in this. . .
> The lonely woman who must toil
> From morn till eve,
> Before a morsel hits her teeth
> Or a drop of water cools her throat.
>
> *2nd Woman*: My sister, you are not alone.
> But who would have thought that I,
> Whose house is teeming with children.
> My own, my husband's, my sister's . . .
> But this is my curse. . . .
> I am telling you, my sister,
> Sometimes we feel you are luckier
> Who are childless.
>
> *1st Woman*: But at the very last
> You are the luckiest who have them.
> Take Esi Kom, I say. (5)

There is great irony in this passage because on one hand, it is a curse in traditional African culture to be childless, so it is hard to believe the 2nd Woman's statement that the childless woman is luckier; yet, on the other hand, Esi Kom, who exemplifies the statement that women with children are luckier, is to suffer the consequences of an ungrateful child. The conversation of these two women sets up a communal perspective on the events they are to narrate by bringing the audience into the argument of "who is luckier" and by focusing on what the community expects of its female citizens.

As storytellers, the two women are constantly acting as the liaisons between the audience and the players. Not only do they express (as ethical advisors) the community's demands on women even when these demands are in opposition to their own individual desires, but as the tellers of the tale, they also guide the audience, so that the audience will focus on the major issues to be discussed later. The two women are constantly directing the audience's attention to important moral and social issues. In the middle of Act Five, for example, the two women have been wakened by strange sounds and meet each other in the path between the houses. The 1st Woman comments, "Is this noise not enough to wake the dead? / Why so much noise at midnight?" The 2nd Woman answers, "It is very dark. / I cannot make out the figure at the door, / It looks like a . . . ghost" (46). Of course, it is Ato who has been hysterically looking for his wife who has run away after a quarrel. But our narrators, besides making sure that the audience responds to the social issues being presented, are also there to insure we make another connection, already hinted at in the play—Ato's own dilemma is symbolized by the ghost's.

The two women have different points of view toward the action of the play, mostly because of their ability to have children—one barren, one fertile. Dapo Adelugba suggests that "their two different perspectives are again the playwright's way of ensuring audience interest and involvement" (77). Indeed, that is part of their role as storytellers. But the fact that their different perspectives revolve around the issue of childlessness also reflects Aidoo's intention to focus on the position of women in the society. As the community voice, they—like the women in Efuru's village—maintain and pass on traditions which are often not to their own advantage. At the beginning of Act Two, the two women address Esi Kom's predicament and whether or not Ato is helping his family to pay back for all the expense of his education (he is not). The 1st Woman, who is childless and suffers from this misfortune, still reinforces the values of "child wealth": "Child bearing is always profitable / For were not our fathers wise / Who looked upon the motion of your lives / And said, / They ask for the people of the house / and not the money in it?" (16). As I mentioned in the chapter on *Efuru*, what the "fathers" have said has been passed on from mother to daughter, emphasizing the necessity for children in opposition to women's rights and happiness because "even from bad marriages / Are born good sons and daughters" (17).

Their discussion of Eulalie's supposed childlessness also illustrates this dialectic and how some women can maintain the position of the community while personally sympathizing with those who cannot fit into the prescribed patterns. Their conversation at the beginning of Act Four is, for the most part, comic, expressing disbelief and disgust at the fact that Eulalie (the stranger girl) has to use "machines" for everything, and therefore, the young marrieds cannot help support their family. This scorn for Western gadgetry is exaggerated until the 1st Woman (barren) asks if Eulalie is "pregnant with a machine child?" (35). The 2nd Woman, who *knows everything* because she has "born eleven from her womb," pronounces that Eulalie is as barren "as an orange which has been scooped of all fruit." Up until this point, Eulalie has been seen as a subject of ridicule, and the coldness of the women as authorities on community standards is evident. But after the 2nd Woman, who is secure within the culture's expectations, leaves, the 1st Woman gives one of the most poignant speeches in the play, empathizing with what she thinks is Eulalie's plight:

> If it is real barrenness
> Then, oh stranger girl . . .
> I weep for you
> For I know what it is
> To start a marriage with barrenness. . . .
> Your machines, my stranger-girl
> Cannot go on an errand
> They have no hands to dress you when you are dead. . .
> But you have one machine to buy now
> That which will weep for you, stranger girl
> You need that most.
> For my world
> Which you have run to enter
> Is most unkind to the barren. (36)

The 1st Woman's painful speech prepares us for the climax of the play, where the family members want to "wash" Eulalie's stomach to cure her barrenness; but more importantly, the 1st Woman's sympathy for Eulalie also prepares us for the eventual acceptance of Eulalie, the lost daughter, into the house of Esi Kom. Some critics have seen the final reconciliation between Esi Kom and Eulalie as "unconvincing," but there are incidents in the play, like the speech quoted above, which show the solidarity of women as well as Aidoo's specific concern for the reconciliation of all the children of the diaspora.[4]

Akan culture, as part of Black African culture in general, is one "in which the most bonding ties [are] with kin rather than with spouses. . . . Heterosexual conflicts in Ghana, then, reflect more than just the battle of the sexes" (Vellenga 145). Although, as the African-American section of this study illustrates, extended kinship bonds are generally greater among Black Americans than in mainstream white America, there is clearly a conflict between Eulalie's sense of privacy and the Africans' belief that marriage is a communal affair. In the Odumna family, many people made the decision concerning Ato's education, so they never imagined that they would not be involved with his marriage choice. At this point, however, I am not going to focus on Ato's problems but on the generations of women whose advice and response he seems to ignore.

The major kinswomen involved in the marital/cultural conflict between Ato, Eulalie, and his family are Esi Kom, Monka, her daughter, and the grandmother, Nana. In addition, the aunts and uncles are active in the dialogue and decision making. Just as Eulalie has preconceived ideas about her African inlaws, this new family suffers under misconceptions about their new daughter-in-law; moreover, they exhibit a sort of amnesia concerning the effects of the slave trade. But in each situation, Ato, rather than helping them understand, thwarts their efforts. Nana represents the oldest generation and is the voice of wisdom, in tune with the ancestors, even if her voice is a little befuddled with age. Her place in the family is a microcosm of the role of the older woman in Akan society: "Among older women, the child rearing period of their lives being almost over, marriage has become less important, and once again, they orient themselves towards the matrilineage and their roles as grandmothers and maternal aunts" (Abu 159). Nana is well past childbearing age, so her concerns are on imparting the traditions to the family. The fact that Ato is unable to converse with her shows his disinterest in the language and culture of his forebears (7). She is one of the venerable women storytellers who "pass on the family history and who know who is kin to whom" (Hill-Lubin 263). On hearing that Eulalie is Black but has no tribe, Nana responds questioningly: "Since I was born, I have not heard of a human being born out from the womb of a woman who has no tribe. *Are there trees which never have any roots?*" (11; emphasis added). The issue of the loss of "roots" and reidentification of culture is paramount for the writers in the African-American section of this study. For Nana, who has never known that kind of separation, not having a tribe is like not having a mother, family, life. In trying to explain, Ato tells her and the rest of the family that Eulalie's antecedents were the Africans brought to the Americas as slaves. When he tries to amend what he has said to stop the family uproar, he makes it worse by saying that only her grandparents were slaves. In a culture which believes that the ancestors are always close at hand, his comment does not reassure them. Nana stops him with, "Ato, do not talk with the foolishness of your generation" (130). Her reaction to Ato shows her and the other family members' inability to deal with the memory of the slave trade, but it also illustrates her fear of losing the lines that tie her to her own ancestors and descendants. Her invocation at the end of Act One reflects this fear of the tradition breaking down as it raises a question for the audience to ponder: "My spirit Mother ought to have come for me earlier. / Now what shall I tell them who are gone? The daughter / of slaves who came from the white man's land. / Someone should advise me on how to tell my story" (14). Nana is a link between the ancestors and future generations; her inability to tell the story correctly to her ancestors because of Ato's silence endangers her role as ethical advisor to the children and as spokeswoman to the ancestors. But her own culture's refusal to face up to the facts of the slave trade also limits her voice.

Esi Kom, the mother, and her daughter Monka are the other important women characters, and it is they who come in direct confrontation with Eulalie. Although the focus of the following discussion will be on Esi Kom, Monka is closely bound not only to the generation of women in her family but also to the oral voicings of her foremothers. When Eulalie throws away the delicacies--snails--that Esi Kom has brought them, Monka sings a folk song to express her anger at her sister-in-law: "She is strange, / She is unusual. / She would have done murder / Had she been a man. / But to prevent / Such an outrage / They made her a woman!" (29).

Esi Kom, who has suffered slights from her son and insults from her daughter-in-law, understands Monka's anger but holds her peace until the climax. Esi Kom is the most significant person in the play because she spans oceans and generations to bring about a reconciliation with her Black American daughter-in-law. As I noted in the introduction, the mother is the central link in both African and African-American family systems; this may be even more pronounced in a matrilineal system such as the Akan. This is evident in *The Dilemma of a Ghost* since Esi Kom is the primary moving force in the play. In the course of the play, Esi Kom puts up with a lot from her son and daughter-in-law, and the plight of the family, narrated by the two women, always centers on Esi Kom's distress (very much like the children in Efuru's compound who center on the "mother" of the proud girl in the folk tale). It is Esi Kom who has to live in the clan house because her son has not built her one (6); she is the one who suffers because her son has not helped her to repay the debts incurred in his schooling. Furthermore, neither Ato nor Eulalie will accept her role as ethical advisor to the new daughter-in-law so that she can teach Eulalie the customs and traditions of the culture. When she and Monka visited them in Accra, the two kinswomen were not welcomed: "I had thought I would do as other women do—spend one or two days with my daughter-in-law, teach her how to cook your favorite meals. But as if I was not noticing it, neither you nor your wife bothered to give us seats to sit on or water to cool our parched throats" (30). It is easier to understand Eulalie's breach of hospitality than Ato's. Eulalie is a stranger to the society and, throughout the play, has been rather coolly received by her in-laws. Furthermore, she has received no support whatsoever from her husband in understanding what is expected of her, so she becomes more and more frustrated. But Ato is not ignorant of his culture, although at times during the play, he acts so; rather, he appears ashamed of his cultural traditions as well as his family members, and this adds to Eulalie's own misconceptions.

Eulalie is the one character most misinterpreted by critics of the play.[5] She takes the blame for all the cultural insensitivity in the play and is seen as arrogant, alcoholic, and obtuse, in spite of the fact that the other characters have their own prejudices and add to hers. Aidoo herself comments that "this play sparked off a whole lot of controversy because people always cling to it looking for something negative about the Black American girl" (Vincent 4). She goes on to say that she is "harsh" on all the characters involved—educated Africans, traditional Africans, and Black Americans—but if one looks closely, it is really Ato who receives the harshest criticism, since he is the one character excluded from the final reconciliation. Aidoo's portrayal of Eulalie is not a negative one, in spite of Eulalie's obvious breaches of cultural sensitivity; rather it is a sympathetic portrait of the "double-self" image of the Black American, explored by W. E. B. DuBois, being both/neither "American" and "African."[6] Ato is hardly being candid with Eulalie when he states that there is no reason for them to have children right away: "'Lalie, don't you believe me when I tell you it's O.K. . . . . Children, who wants them? In fact, they will make me jealous. I couldn't bear seeing you love someone else better than you do me" (4). Besides being totally dishonest to Eulalie about what is going to be expected of her when she arrives in Ghana, Ato ignores a family system which believes that "a woman's role as wife is secondary to her role as mother" (Kilson, "Women and African Literature" 165). Eulalie expresses the same concern later, but Ato responds once again with false platitudes so that the situation ends up exploding in the climax of the play.

Eulalie's misconceptions as well as her strong desire to finally "belong" are understandable. Before she meets Ato's family, she hopes not only to be part of his family but of his people, asking if she can adopt them as her own (3–4). Eulalie's lament reflects her feelings of isolation as a second-class American citizen and her desire for a real family, and it also illustrates Eulalie's notion of extended family, which possibly stems from her African heritage. Eulalie's identification with her African heritage is further illustrated in her monologue at the beginning of Act Two. Although this speech is full of ill-conceived prejudices carried over from American films and television, it exposes some of the similarities she shares with her African family in contradistinction to many of her white American counterparts. At first she states flippantly that she finds all this "rather cute." But her tone becomes increasingly serious when she remembers the hardships faced at home and the death of all those close to her. She is enheartened by the thought of her dead mother's presence; she speaks to her mother of her accomplishments, keeping the lines between generations, living and dead, alive: "Ma, I've come to the very source. I've come to Africa and I hope that where'er you are, you sort of know and approve" (19). Because of her belief in returning to the "source," her understanding of an extended family, and her communication with her dead mother, Eulalie might have blended in more easily with her new family and culture, had she any help from her husband. Since Ato is the only one to have lived on both sides of the Atlantic, he should be the one to smooth over the problems, but instead he exacerbates them. With his lack of initiative, the animosity between Eulalie and Esi Kom's family moves toward open hostility in the climax of the play.

The climax comes when the family—aunts and uncles, Monka, Esi Kom, and Nana—comes to Ato to find out what is preventing him from giving his grandmother "a great-grandchild before she leaves us" (40). They have brought medicine to wash Eulalie's stomach so that she can become fertile. Ato not only refuses their help but fails to explain to the family that he and Eulalie have been using birth control. The elders' belief in the traditional values is shaken as Esi Kom tells them that "these days, one's son's marriage affair cannot be always one's affair" (39). But Nana, the mainstay of the tradition, knocks her stick on the ground and states: "It may be so in many homes. Things have not changed here." Eulalie, who asks Ato why he doesn't tell them the truth, realizes that she, too, has been duped by him, she comments bitterly: "You knew all this, didn't you, my gallant Black knight? Now you dare not confess it before them . . ." (42). In this argument, she finally directs a question to Ato, which should have been broached long before and which has a broad meaning for the audience: "Who married me, you or your goddamn people?" (44).

Ironically, it is precisely because Eulalie has married a family as well as a person that there can be any reconciliation in this play. Even though major aspects of traditional life in African communities have changed because of the influx of Western culture, much has survived; moreover, it is the women who have attempted to keep aspects of the traditional world alive in daily life, a world with strong family ties and community resources. And even for Eulalie, this world will protect her since, with the family's growing awareness of Ato's duplicity, she is no longer seen as a villain but as a lost child. "In the end, or so the play implies, [Eulalie] may find a truer freedom and womanhood within African collectivity. African ways are envisioned as life-giving" (Chapman 33). In the final confrontation between Esi Kom and her son Ato, the play makes a stand for

African womanhood, the lost children of the diaspora, and the importance of familial ties and community traditions. It also questions an education which appears to be learned out of context, learned only to deny the knowledge of generations. Esi Kom attacks her son because he seems to "never know anything" in spite of his education. When he starts speaking about the new inventions in "these days of civilization," she exclaims, "In these days of civilization, what? Now I know you have been teaching your wife to insult us. . . . No stranger ever breaks the law . . . my son. You have not dealt with us well. And you have not dealt with your wife well in this" (49). At this point Eulalie, hurt and exhausted, stumbles in, and Esi Kom, rather than Ato, rushes to support her. The symbolism is unmistakable; Esi Kom reaches out not only to her daughter-in-law but to Eulalie's dead mother, oceans and generations away, who is watching:

> And we must be careful with your wife
> You tell us her mother is dead.
> If she had any tenderness,
> Her ghost must be keeping watch over
> All which happens to her . . .
> [*There is short silence, then clearly to Eulalie,*]
> Come, my child. (50)

The reconciliation of Esi Kom and Eulalie reflects, on a personal level, a coming home for those in the diaspora as well as a move toward recognition of a "grief accepted and overcome" for those in Africa. Esi Kom's acceptance of Eulalie also implies the acceptance of the entire Yawson family, and probably of the community (illustrated, at least, by the sympathies of the 1st Woman narrator). At the end of the play, Ato, alienated, is alone on the stage, hearing nothing but the echo of the song which repeats his dilemma.

As in all dilemma tales, the problems exposed in *The Dilemma of a Ghost* are not solved, although the play does give us a moral "last word" on the dilemma of traditional versus Western values and the acceptance of the total past of a people, the positive *and* negative aspects. The play does not neatly resolve the issue of how modern Africans are to synthesize their Western learning with the traditional wisdom of the past generations, nor does it attempt to reconcile the fact of a diaspora with the millions of disinherited peoples who have evolved into other cultures; furthermore, it does not solve the problem women face in passing on cultural traditions which often limit their own roles as members of the community. But the play does give some personal answers to the questions raised; moreover, its ending leaves open these questions and ethical judgments so that the audience, reader, and listener can debate, discuss, and come to conclusions for themselves.

# II

# *The African-Americans*

■

*The first section of this book explored the role of the African woman and African woman writer as a domestic and master storyteller, tied to the oral traditions of her culture, who imparts the values of her culture to her children and children's children. These values affirm a primary relationship and responsibility to one's entire extended family, an emphasis on the needs of the community (at times in opposition to individual needs), the predominance of "people" over "things," and the importance of childbearing and raising as part of a lineage which continues from the ancestors to the unborn. This sense of generational continuity pervades all other values and is deeply rooted in the prescribed role of the African woman.*

*In the following section, I examine how the African-American woman has cultivated the traditions of her African foremothers by passing on her culture's history and values in the orature and how three writers—Alice Walker, Toni Morrison, Paule Marshall—evoke generational and cultural continuity in the telling of the tale. In each of the novels examined, the protagonist moves from a life of fragmentation and isolation to a (re)vision of wholeness and sense of community through an acceptance of his/her African-based heritage. In each situation, the protagonist learns of this heritage through at least one mothering character—an elder, ancestor, or significant other. In a self-reflexive process of reformulating the tales and traditions of their foremothers, the three novelists continue their role as African-American women storytellers to pass on the values and heritage of their culture to future generations.*

# 4

## Alice Walker,
## *The Color Purple*

The artist then is the voice of the people,
but she is also The People.

Alice Walker

■ In the first section of this study, I examined the writings of three African women as part of their aim to pass on their cultural traditions to future generations, to reflect and often to reform their culture. On this side of the Atlantic, Alice Walker, novelist, short-story writer, poet, essayist, and political activist, has been an un-flinching proponent of "usable" art in an Afrocentric context—art that is not separated from the people or the community from whence it was derived, that reflects the community's his/herstory, and that reforms the community's traditions and values for the col-lective health of the people. The history of Black America has in-cluded violent attacks on the community's health, from the initial iniquity of slavery to modern day racism and the imposition of dominant cultural values and ideals. As a writer, activist, and "womanist," Walker has directed her energies to expose both the richness and destruction in the Black community, particularly in relation to its women; moreover, she has emphasized the necessity of understanding one's past so as to be able to pass it on to future generations.[1] She was in the forefront in renewing interest in Har-lem Renaissance writer Zora Neale Hurston, a spiritual foremother for many contemporary Black American writers.[2] In speaking about Hurston, she details what she feels is the duty of the Black writer:

"*We are a people. A people do not throw their geniuses away*. And if they are thrown away, it is our duty *as artists and as witnesses for the future* to collect them again for the sake of our children, and, if necessary, bone by bone" (*In Search of Our Mothers' Gardens* 92; italics in original). Her duty to preserve past geniuses for the children does not end with specific artists but includes all of the anonymous, creative mother/grandmother artists who lived to allow writers like Hurston and Walker to bloom. Other examples of Walker's attention to her culture's "geniuses"—both known and unknown— are her teaching of Black woman's herstory, her literacy work, her essays and speeches, and most importantly, her fiction.

In her works, Walker has "minded" her culture—as sister-storyteller Sutherland calls it—both the African and African-American aspects of it; she has underscored the folk heritage which has helped African-American culture to survive. In this chapter I discuss *The Color Purple* (1982); I concentrate on Walker's aim to explore the African part of her cultural heritage, particularly in rural Southern Black life, and her aim to bring to light the positive values of her culture's unique Afrocentric qualities. A major aspect of African cultural survivals and a motif in Walker's writing is the return to the extended family, violently broken and distorted by the historical circumstances of African-American life—a progression from her early work *The Third Life of Grange Copeland* to *The Color Purple*. I focus on Walker's position as a descendant of the African woman storyteller and her debt to African and African-American foremothers, women's significant role in the revitalization of African family organization through consanguinal and community kin, and her utopian recreation of an African village compound at the end of the novel. Moreover, as in Aidoo's play, this study examines the conflicts in the relationship between those from Africa and those from the diaspora—African values as distinct from Africa. Walker, who calls herself "author and medium," conjures up her ancestors to pass on the lives, stories, and traditions to "those blameless hostages we leave to the future, our children" (*Mothers' Gardens* 120).[3]

Like her African sister-storytellers, Walker passes on the orature of her foremothers to the children and recreates the stories of her own mother in her writings. Celie, the main character of *The Color Purple*, is based on Walker's great-grandmother; furthermore, Walker's desire to give her foremothers credit is clearly reflected in her essays: "And so our mothers and grandmothers have, more often than not anonymously, handed on the creative spark, the seed of the flower they themselves never hoped to see . . ." (*Mothers' Gardens* 240). Walker does not see herself unique in this attention to her mothers' stories nor in the urgency needed to pass on these tales and traditions so that they will not be lost in the glare of the television; when she says "our," she is referring to the other Black women (writers) who have also discerned their debt to their foremothers and who strive to reproduce the "historical collective experience of all Black women" (Rodgers-Rose 9). Until *The Temple of My Familiar, The Color Purple* was Walker's most realized work in terms of her aim to incorporate African heritage and family organization in her novels,[4] but a few examples show that she has been working toward this objective since she started writing. Her first novel, *The Third Life of Grange Copeland* (1970), illustrates the breakdown of the extended family under the strains of poverty and racial oppression, yet within the novel are the seeds of hope for a more integrated African-American society based on African values and oral traditions. The most positive relationship in the book is between the grandfather Grange (who was a horror as a young man) and his grandchild Ruth. Disgusted by the education Ruth receives at school, Grange teaches her about her culture through the stories and folk tales from the time of slavery and before. In this case, the one who tells the tale is an old man—Ruth's mother having been murdered by Grange's son–yet the tradition of passing down the stories to future generations–remains.

By the time Walker writes *Meridian* (1976), her emphasis is almost completely on women's role in passing on one's African heritage, although one recipient is a man. Meridian, a tale teller herself, has problems with her own mother but gains strength from her mother's story; moreover, Meridian's duty, as an informant for her family, is to pass on the history of all her foremothers so that their creativity will not have been wasted. Walker's most pointed instance of women-identified storytelling comes from the legend Meridian hears about a woman slave from West Africa whose family practice was the "weaving of intricate tales with which to entrap people who hoped to get away with murder" (42). Of course a woman slave with that calling was not going to last long in a society bent on her dehumanization, and eventually she is punished by having her tongue cut out. Here the silencing of both Black and female experience is graphically rendered. In resistance, the slave

Louvinie keeps the tongue because in her native African tradition: "Without one's tongue in one's mouth or in a special spot of one's own choosing, the singer in one's soul was lost forever to grunt and snort through eternity like a pig" (44). This legend, similar to the Greek myth of Procne and Philomela, is clearly symbolic of the necessity of keeping and placing the songs and stories of value into the right ears. Without the stories, the singer in one's soul will be lost.

In *The Color Purple*, Walker strives to recreate the orature of her ancestors as oraliterature. The novel is epistolary, and this private form of communication evokes a sense of the orality of the stories to the reader. The letters are written as the main character Celie speaks—in dialect—so we get a sense of conversation, of words coming through the voice rather than on the page. In addition, her letters are rarely descriptive; they recall complete discussions of events as well as statements directed to the recipient of the letters, whether it is God or Celie's sister Nettie. The first letters, as early attempts of literary voicings, reflect a literacy just conquered, and one close to its oral roots. Celie's letters are imbued with the oral traditions and forms of her community's voice, and unlike the expected dominance of literature over orature, for Celie and the reader, "oral expression is no longer subjugated by written expression" (Babb 107). Instead of feeling encumbered by the dense, "literary" form of the traditional novel, we experience Celie's story through the oral voicings of letters. In Celie's first letter to God, the orality of Walker's writing style is audible: "He never had a kine word to say to me. Just say You gonna do what your mammy wouldn't. . . . He start to choke me, saying You better shut up and get used to it" (1). Celie speaks out to God as if the spirit is in the room with her, explaining her pregnancy from the rape by her supposed father, and then asking God to help her understand her circumstances. Since to tell anyone else would "kill her mammy," Celie's only choice is to *talk* to God.

The fact that the letters Celie writes are never read by the person/spirit intended sets up an interesting dialectic in the novel's structure. Celie's first letters are written to God, and we can safely assume that they are, at least, never answered. Her later letters to her sister Nettie, after she finds out that Nettie is alive and in Africa, are never received. The only letters read are Nettie's to Celie, and these are found long after they were written. Evidently, Walker is suggesting a limitation to literacy and the passing on of stories through a written medium; the stories, with the exception of Nettie's to Celie, are exchanged verbally by the characters, and only the reader gets the version written in the letter. But the apparent break of communication by the unread letters is undermined by the fact that the reader acts as the liaison, knowing each person's story and how the tales relate to each other. S/he actively participates in this collective experience, a function of African as well as women's art, and takes with her/him the stories which have been passed on through the characters to the reader. As King-Kok Cheung notes in "Imposed Silences in *The Color Purple* and *The Woman Warrior*," "The unspoken or unheard testimonies become powerful indictments on the written page" (164).

But there is a caveat implied here. Walter Ong in *Orality and Literacy* comments:

> Written words are residue. The oral tradition has no such residue or deposit. When an often told story is not actually being told, all that exists of it is the potential in certain human beings to tell it.... Fortunately literacy, though it consumes its own oral antecedents and, *unless it is carefully monitored even destroys their memory*, is also infinitely adaptable. (11; 15; emphasis added)

The warning is that literacy as a hegemonic mode cannot preserve the flavor and richness of the oral tradition, and it appears that Walker is echoing this concern. The letters that Celie writes, although they manage to adapt and reform the oral tradition, are in the end unread by those to whom she writes. Yet, since the letters are read by the reader who learns Celie's and the other ancestors' stories, the literature itself becomes oraliterature—a means to bridge the gap between oral and written traditions; moreover, the passage of the letters also illustrates a potential mending of the historical gap of the Middle Passage. Still, in the same manner as her African sister-storytellers, Walker emphasizes that the tales, values, and traditions of African-American culture may be lost if not passed on in orature as well.

Like Flora Nwapa, Alice Walker returns to the rural life of her people to focus on the traditions and values that have been passed on, but as Sutherland and Aidoo have done, she also works toward reforming her culture by presenting a vision of a more integrated

African-American society. In this way, Walker functions as ethical advisor as well as storyteller, for she feels that "the saving of lives" is what writers should be all about (*Mothers' Gardens* 14). In much of her writings, the characters' lives are saved by a return to the extended family—African family organization—which has been distorted and disrupted by the effects of poverty, racism, and the pressure to conform to white society's dominant cultural values and nuclear family structure. The progression from the violent absence of an extended family system to the recreation of an African model of a village compound in *The Color Purple* follows the pattern of Walker's development from her dissection of violence and oppression in *The Third Life of Grange Copeland* to her Afro-utopian vision, heralding a change, in *The Color Purple* (this vision expands toward a global community in *Temple*). Celie, our letter-writer, has been called "a Mem [Ruth's mother in *The Third Life of Grange Copeland*, whose husband blows her head off with a shotgun] who survives and liberates herself" (Christian, "The Black Woman Artist" 470), and her story invokes strength for future generations of Black women.

Celie's story is extraordinary, although I cannot agree with Trudier Harris that it is an "incredible" one (156), at least not in the context of this utopian novel. The first letter of the novel, quoted above, explains Celie's pregnancy from the repeated rape by her father (actually, her stepfather). To save her sister Nettie from the same fate, Celie arranges for her to become a governess to a missionary couple who have adopted Celie's two illegitimate children. The rest of the novel takes place in both Africa and the rural South, exploring, on one hand, Nettie's impressions of African culture and society and, on the other, Celie's suffering and growth through the recreation of her extended family, specifically her relationship with her husband's lover, the blues singer Shug Avery.

The novel opens with a glimpse at a family which seems to have no family organization—African or Euro-American. The family has no extended kin, no cohesive value system, and no relationships except those based solely on abuse. The women are victimized, and Celie and Nettie's mother, overburdened, overworked, and forced into having too many children without any familial support, is not able to fulfill her maternal duties to her two daughters by an earlier marriage. Celie's ignorance about the sexual act and its outcome further illustrates her mother's lack of maternal guidance. When her mother dies, Celie is left to take care of the other children and succumb to her stepfather. But Celie does not blame her mother for what happens, for as she tells God, "Maybe cause my mama cuss me you think I kept mad at her. But I aint. I felt sorry for her. Trying to believe his story kilt her" (15). The stories that should have been passed on from mother to daughter are lost to the wicked lies of her stepfather. His intervention disrupts generational/cultural continuity. Celie intuitively feels the deprivation she has had to face without a mother, but she realizes much later how this loss has stunted her emotional/spiritual growth. As another Walker character says, "Mothers, she learned very soon, were a premium commodity" (*Third Life* 188), and if a child, like Celie, didn't have one, she was considered the poorest of the poor. As illustrated in the African section, the importance of maternal guidance and maternal love (coming from any/all mothers in the kinship network) cannot be overestimated. Celie and her sister Nettie are not only without a mother but without any elder, grandparent, or significant other; therefore, the kind of abuse that Celie suffers from her supposed father goes unchecked. Without any extended family system, Celie has to take on the role of "mother" to her sister, and she manages to protect Nettie from the advances of Pa; ironically, it is Celie's acceptance of sexual abuse which allows Nettie to remain unscathed. As sociologist Wilhelmina Manns notes, "The older sibling has been more critical to Black family life than has been recognized" (245). Their immediate family—which is reduced to the clinging of two scared sisters—exemplifies the total breakdown of the extended family organization and exposes their vulnerability and isolation from their heritage and the community around them.

Joyce Ladner, in her ground-breaking study of adolescent girls growing up in Black America, comments, "Life in the Black community has been conditioned by poverty, discrimination, and institutional subordination. It has also been shaped by African cultural survivals" (*Tomorrow's Tomorrow* 12). Although it has been conjectured that the system of slavery reinforced the primary unit of mother-child, other aspects of slavery disrupted African family organization. Under slavery, parents were not able to exercise authority over their children, which is an important aspect of any family unit, and families were constantly split up. But in spite of the opposition, extended family members were able "oftentimes to impart certain values and cultural ethos to their offsprings" (Ladner, "Racism and

Tradition" 276). So throughout generations, African values and family organization have continued from the first Africans in slavery, although these lifestyles have been often disrupted and imposed upon by "poverty, discrimination and institutional subordination." In *The Color Purple*, it is evident that the seeds of the residual extended family system remain with the two sisters and, as the novel progresses, Celie and Nettie join with the other women—sisters-in-law, significant others, "co-wives"—and the men they live with to rebuild an extended family structure which allows them freedom to grow. The kinship ties utilized to rebuild the extended family in this novel are based on two types of bonds; neither is conjugal (that is the most suspect of all kinship ties). The first is the consanguinal bond of sibling, parent-child, family kin; the second is what I will call "community" ties which include in-laws, lovers, "the other women" and their children. These community ties tend to revolve around the bonding and solidarity of women, often in spite of the opposition of their male lovers, husbands, and kin.

The most important familial bond in the novel is between the sisters, Celie and Nettie. Their attachment and devotion to each other remains constant despite male intrusion and geographical distance. When Nettie leaves for Africa with the missionaries, Celie has no knowledge of her sister's whereabouts. It is only after Shug, Celie's husband's lover, reveals to her that Albert has been hiding all of Nettie's letters that Celie is able to piece together Nettie's story (114). The finding of Nettie's letters effects two major changes in the novel. First, it is the beginning of the woman-identified bonding of Celie and Shug, which I explore later in the chapter. Second, after Celie has an address for Nettie, she stops writing to God and begins to write to her sister. This change not only separates her from a "trifling" God but further focuses her communication toward the intimacy of women together, sisters.

Although the emphasis in this novel concerns woman-identified bonding between kin and non-kin, there are two instances of familial bonding which include men. I mention these here since they have been largely ignored by male critics who have attacked the book for its portrayal of the Black male. The first instance concerns Celie's relationship to her stepfather and father. Through the help of both Nettie and Shug, Celie finds out that "Pa" is not her father and that her children, although products of rape, are not from an incestuous assault. Furthermore, she finds out that her father was a brave, kind, and courageous man, unlike the cruel, immoral, egotistical Pa. Her father, a successful small businessman, was too successful for his white competition, so they lynched him and burned his store. Nettie explains in a letter that when his wife (their mother) saw her husband's body brought home "mutilated and burnt," she was never the same (161). This understanding gives Celie peace of mind not only concerning her children's health but also about her mother's apparent inability to nurture. Moreover, it locates the source of oppression within the system which designed it. By this acknowledgment and the search for her parents' graves with Shug (167), Celie recovers her parents, and through them, a line to her ancestors. The other example of familial bonding relates to a male version of the movement toward an acceptance of family, in this case, Albert (Mr.——) and his son, Harpo. Both men, following in a negative continuum from Albert's father, treat their wives—Celie and Sophia—cruelly, and there is much resentment between father and son. Yet as the novel progresses, Harpo begins to accept Sophia's independence and sees his position in the extended family more clearly. It is Harpo who helps Albert to lose some of his "meanness" by forcing Albert to send Celie Nettie's letters and by giving him filial love (201).

The strongest bonds in the novel, however, recreate African extended family organization in an African-American structure. They are what I call "community" ties—neither consanguinal nor conjugal, although these ties do include lovers of one's husband and in-laws. This bonding is always that of women, as "mates," co-wives, and sisters/daughters-in-law. This community of women is a residual African model of the village compound, where all the women are in charge of all the children, and domestic as well as economic duties are often shared. It is an African-American formulation of woman-identified community structures witnessed in Nwapa's *Efuru*. The friendship between Celie and her daughter-in-law, Sophia, is one example of woman-identified familial bonding. Sophia has many characteristics associated with an African concept of womanhood: She is physically strong, proud, and extremely independent, and she is not embarrassed or the least bit ashamed to be pregnant and not married (38). Furthermore, she has a large, closely knit family, full of siblings and children, with brothers and sisters who are as strong and proud as she. She and her sisters are called "Amazons"; they all have children and share the responsibilities of taking care of them (69). Sophia and her family's attitude about her unborn child reflect an African attitude to childbirth which has been mirrored in the Black American rural community—that "there is an inherent value that children cannot be 'illegally' born" (Ladner, *Tomorrow* 214). The importance of having a child often outweighs the "unauthorized" conception, and the family is generally happy with their "childwealth."

In the course of Celie's friendship with Sophia, Celie learns how to stand up for herself. At first, Celie is intimidated by Sophia's independence and the possibility of intimacy, so when Harpo suggests to Celie that he should beat Sophia to make her "mind," Celie—who understands abuse as the only relationship between men and women—agrees. Celie is ashamed of her actions and is relieved when Sophia confronts her. Their bonding is symbolized in the quilt that they make, "Sister's Choice" (64). By learning from Sophia's example, the continuity of the strong "womanist" quality of her family's women, Celie is able not only to speak up for herself but also to defend Sophia when she needs bolstering.

For non-Africans, a most intriguing aspect of this woman-identified community bonding is the ability of the women in *The Color Purple* to share a husband and still get along (although there is much evidence to suggest that polygyny in African families does not always produce smooth-running households). There are two such relationships in the novel—Sophia and Squeak (wife and lover of Harpo) and Celie and Shug (wife and lover of Albert). Sophia, estranged from husband Harpo, and his "yellow" girlfriend Squeak (Mary Agnes) have all the expected hostility at first. The antagonism escalates at Harpo's Juke joint with Sophia knocking two of Squeak's teeth out (83). Nonetheless, when Sophia is sent to jail for "sassing" the white mayor, Squeak takes care of Sophia's children and succumbs sexually to her white uncle, the warden, to get Sophia out (89-91). By the end of the novel, Squeak and Sophia have each taken care of the other's children by Harpo, and in the last letter, they are together as mates, making potato salad (250).

The most important polygynous and woman-identified relationship is that of Celie and Shug Avery, the blues singer. What Celie learns from Sophia is intensified in her relationship with her lover, Shug. Shug is hardly a traditional role model for Celie; she is Celie's husband's lover. She is not a relation or even a co-wife at the beginning nor is she an elder in the community, the role model most respected in traditional African societies. This is clearly an African-American adaptation of the extended family organization, restructured by slavery, oppression, and the general constraints of American life, especially for women. In Shug, the concept of the "significant other" is realized.[5] Celie and Shug perform this role of significant other for each other, taking on the "parental roles—nurturing—through the mode of emotional support," although the effects are more obviously visible in Celie (Manns 249). Like Sophia, Shug is strong, powerful, independent, "womanish"; moreover, she is economically secure and in total control of her finances. She is also very dark-skinned (seen as a line more directly drawn to her African ancestry). When Celie first sees a picture of Shug, she is captivated by it, seeing Shug as the image of beauty and freedom. She tells God, "An now when I dream, I dream of Shug Avery. She be dressed to kill, whirling and laughing" (16). But when Shug comes to the house to stay, she is not very nice to Celie. Celie, though, mothers Shug through her sickness, and they become sisters, mother/daughter, women together. In Celie's care, Shug is reminded of her grandmother's love and feels closer to the mother who disapproved of her; furthermore, Celie's attention helps Shug create and refine her music while Celie combs her hair: "Something come to me, she say. Something I made up, Something you help scratch out my head" (57). But it is Shug who teaches Celie about life, herself, and her body.

The sexual love relationship between Shug and Celie is the focal point of the novel, and it is through this woman-identified bonding that we see Celie's real growth. Celie, who has seen herself only through the eyes of men, has no respect for her body since it appears to her as "ugly," an object for abuse. Through their lovemaking, Shug, as a spiritual mother, teaches Celie to appreciate and love her own body and self. In a sort of personal "initiation ceremony," Shug teaches Celie what she never learned from her own mother—how to find pleasure in one's body and how to give pleasure in return. Celie refers to sleeping with Shug as a "little like sleeping with mama, only I can't hardly remember ever sleeping with her" (110). Shug helps Celie to deal with her past abuse and to feel love within the context of sisterhood:

> She say, I love you, Miss Celie. And then she haul off and kiss me on the mouth. . . .

Then I feel something real soft and wet on my breast, feel like one
of my lost little babies mouth.
Way after a while, I act like a little lost baby too. (109)

Through their sexual love, Shug and Celie bring back all the lost
family that has been denied them by the oppressive racist and sexist
world in which they live. Their love represents an openness to all the
different aspects of women's capacity to nurture. Sexuality and sexual relations between women is not seen as antithetical to familial
relations; rather, they embrace the entire extended family. The men
in their lives are not thrust out of the community: Shug is clearly
open to heterosexual relationships, and Celie, through her love for
Shug, even begins to tolerate Albert. Lesbianism, according to
Elliott Butler-Evans, "becomes an essential aspect of 'womanist'
theory and praxis" (*Race, Gender, and Desire* 169). Most pertinently, lesbian love in this context is not seen in contradistinction to
the desire for children and the necessity of children for the life of the
community; it is, in fact, life-giving.

Through this love and learning experience, the nurturing of each
other, both Celie and Shug reconnect to their maternal ancestors
and find expression for their love of their lost children. Celie comes
to understand her mother and starts to think of those children being
raised by her sister in Africa as really her own. Shug also finds
strength in their bonding and no longer feels alienated from the
community because of her sexual needs. Furthermore, she sets on a
quest to find her own children who had been raised by their grandparents. Through their love, both Celie and Shug come to redefine
and (re)articulate their values in more holistic, familial, and community terms.

Shug supports Celie in more than personal terms, however; with
Shug's help, Celie becomes economically independent, which puts
her on equal footing with her husband, Albert. So when Celie
comes back to their community from Memphis, she no longer is
submissive nor calls Albert "Mr.——." Toward the end of the novel,
Celie and Albert talk about Shug. Albert says that what he loves
about Shug is that she, like Sophia, is "manly—she bound to live her
life and be herself no matter what." Celie counters that if only
Sophia and Shug have it, then it must be "womanly" (236). I would
suggest that the concept of "womanly" not only reflects Walker's
views of what is "womanist" but also comes from a precolonial

African view of women rather than the dependent, pale, pedestaled European model. What is respected, as illustrated in the African chapters, is not blind submission or delicate personage, but an ability to be economically self-sufficient, to have physical and personal strength, and of course, to produce children. In addition to her personal strength, Shug passes on the ability to be financially independent to Celie. Barbara Christian notes that in *The Color Purple*, "Walker challenges [white] society's definition [of women as dependent on men] by presenting women's communities that are sexually and economically independent of men, though not separate from them" (*Black Feminist Criticism* 199). Like the African market women who hold up their economic end of the family, Celie gains strength from the understanding that she is able to transform a domestic skill into a commercial one: "I sit in the dining room making pants after pants. I got pants now in every color and size under the sun. Since us started making pants down home, I ain't been able to stop" (192). Celie's clothes making gives expression to her creativity which was buried during those years of abuse. She designs pants for the women/sisters she loves, and by the end of the novel, the making of pants and shirts becomes a cottage industry to support her extended family compound.

It is Nettie, though, who teaches Celie about her African heritage. The African sections of this novel have caused problems for some of its critics, including myself, for numerous reasons—from their lack of personal voice and integration into the novel's structure to their misrepresentation of West African culture and colonial history.[6] I am concerned about what I consider Walker's misreading of African society and women's role in it. Clearly there is a conflict in Walker's perception of African culture which is apparently in opposition to her attitude toward African heritage. Walker's Western perceptions of African society become increasingly problematic as we witness her emphasis on the "restorative myths of Black hegemony" (Hite 264) and the reclamation of African heritage to build a more integrated African-American society.

Walker has spent time in Africa, yet when she quotes women's opinions exploring their roles in Black Africa in *In Search of Our Mothers' Gardens* (66–70), she cites Nigerian writer Buchi Emecheta (who has often been criticized for a westernized approach to her own culture, especially in her early works). Moreover, in spite of paying lip service to the effects of colonialization, Walker apparently perceives African culture as static; she appears to ignore the fact that the status of the African women she saw in the 1960s (even in a village setting) had been eroded by the patriarchal British system. (Walker does appear to amend this view in *Temple* where she focuses more clearly on the effects of colonialization on traditional African societies.) *The Color Purple* reflects a time when missionaries and government officials were first strengthening their hold on the interior of West Africa, and yet Walker does not take into account the "dual sex role system" examined in the African section. This system of domestic ordering, which emphasized strictly defined and *functional* roles for both sexes, was probably still the dominant mode of gender relations. For example, when one of the African girls in the village wants to go to school to be with her Black American friends, her father does not approve. Nettie tells him, "The world is changing, I said. It is no longer a world just for boys and men" (148). The African world has never been a place just for boys and men; the dual sex role system, although still male-dominated, structured responsibilities for all members of the community. In addition, women held traditional positions of authority in their courts, religious ceremonies, and economic matters. If, then, the only option left for the village girl in a system stripped of its power by colonialism is to go to a Christian school, is this the fault of the African man alone?

This conflict in Walker's appraisal of African culture is even more pronounced in relationship to her desire to build cultural ties between African and African-American women, based on oppression. Butler-Evans states in his study *Race, Gender, and Desire* that the purpose of the letters is to emphasize the history of "the universal oppression of Black women everywhere" (171). But as Butler-Evans points out in "Beyond Essentialism," these binary oppositions can be grossly misleading. For if Black women everywhere are "the mules of the world" to quote Zora Neale Hurston, then how did African-American women gain all that strength, passed down for generations from their African foremothers? I am not suggesting that precolonial West Africa had societies that were totally equitable gender-wise, but in spite of that, the African women were (are) hardly submissive, as shown in the first section of this study. And certain actions that Westerners, like Walker and myself, might see as symbolizing complete subjugation of women may actually be much less telling. For example, Nettie tells Celie:

There is a way men speak to women that reminds me too much of
Pa. . . . They don't even look at women when women are speaking.
They look at the ground and bend their heads towards the ground.
The women also do not 'look in a man's face' as they say. To 'look
in a man's face' is a brazen thing to do. They look instead at his feet
or his knees. (148)

Despite the similarities between African and African-American communities, body language is strongly culture-bound and often does
not have the same meaning. In fact it is quite possible to read this
passage as the man and woman not looking at *each other* to show
mutual respect.[7] We come to believe in Nettie, like Celie, as a
"reliable" narrator, so her visions of Africa appear true; yet comments like her intimation that African men treat their women like
white people treat Blacks perpetuates typical Western prejudices
concerning African society. It is understandable that Walker wants
to build coalitions between Black women of Africa and the diaspora,
but it would seem that the comparison could also be drawn from
another premise—that African-American women have gained their
strength, independence, and notion of song from their African
foremothers.

Notwithstanding the problems of the African sections of the
novel, there are benefits in their inclusion in the text, especially in
terms of Walker's apparent desire to build alliances among those of
African descent as well as uncover residual African culture. Although
described disparagingly by Mel Watkins as "mere monologues on
African history" (7), Nettie's accounts of African life may serve
Walker's polemical purpose of educating not only Celie and the
other characters but also the reader. Walker might have done better
to incorporate these views within the context of rural Southern
Georgia, but as these descriptions stand, they try to correct some of
the negative attitudes within the Black community toward its African past. Nettie tells Celie that there were great cities and empires in
Africa, that the Egyptians were Africans, that Ethiopia in the Bible
was Africa, and, most importantly from a Christian point of view,
that Jesus Christ was "colored" and "had hair like lamb's wool"
(125-26). Moreover, in her letters, Nettie refers to the common
ancestry of African and African-Americans in a discussion of the
slave trade: When Olivia (Celie's daughter) tells her African friend

Tashi about how her great-grandmother was treated as a slave, Tashi cries. But Nettie states further that "no one else in this village wants to hear about slavery, however. They acknowledge no responsibility whatsoever" (152). Like her African sister-storyteller Aidoo, Walker feels that the issue of the slave trade must be addressed by communities on both sides of the Atlantic, so that no part of one's heritage, however painful, should be left out.

Another positive attribute of African culture that Walker brings to light in these sections is the close relationship between women in a polygamous household and in the village setting in general. Nettie witnesses missionary Samuel's confusion because he believes in monogamy but sees the closeness of the women who share their husbands (153). Nettie, whose experiences within monogamous households have been negative, is also sympathetic, and her comments concerning the woman-identified bonding of co-wives foreshadows the Afro-utopian ending of the novel. A final aspect of African culture, illustrated in the African sections and particularly germane to this study, is the manner in which the women impart traditions and tales. The two young girls, Tashi and Olivia, swap folk tales only to find that the Uncle Remus tale that Olivia tells has its "original version" in Tashi's African orature. This scene illustrates how folklore has been passed down by domestic storytellers, as the characters explore generational continuity—"how Tashi's people's stories got to America" (152). Moreover, not only does Nettie listen to the stories of her little African daughter but she passes those stories on to her sister. It is Nettie's recreation of their African heritage which helps Celie to grow into her own person.

By the end of the novel, Celie is one of Walker's "emergent" women because in her life there is a reconciliation with both her cultural heritage and the man she lives with—two of the criteria for the emergent woman (Washington 214). Through the devotion of her sister Nettie, her lover Shug, and the family of women around her, she survives. Walker, in her portrayal of Celie, transforms this story of her own great-grandmother, a slave raped at age twelve by the plantation owner, by giving it a happy ending. Walker comments on this utopian vision in a *Newsweek* interview, "I liberated her from her own history. . . . I wanted her to be happy" (Interview 67). But in a way, this comment is ironic, because in liberating Celie (the great-grandmother) from her history, Walker has given Celie (the character) back her heritage. And like African sister-storyteller Efua

Sutherland, Walker has reformed a family legend into a tale with a positive message: "Let's hope people can hear Celie's voice. There are so many people like Celie who make it, who come out of nothing. People who triumph" (Interview 67).

The end of *The Color Purple* is indeed a utopian vision, and if seen in that light, the fact that this ending is, to some extent, "incredible" is no longer a negative criticism. In fact, the use of a utopian vision by oppressed people has been seen as a counter-hegemonic approach to fighting their oppression.[8] I would suggest further that Walker's utopian vision is Afro-utopian, a vision conceived in the values and traditions of Africa and passed on through generations of African-American folk life. And in spite of the misreading of African society, Walker's vision for a more integrated African-American life runs true to African cultural values adapted from the West African communities from whence the slaves came— that of extended family, community, and kinship ties from the ancestors to the future generations of children; moreover, as Paul Carter Harrison states of his own play, "The Great MacDaddy" in *Kuntu Drama*, "The intention of the ritual, then, is to identify, rather than simulate African sensibilities as perceived in the context of African/Americans" (259). Walker's identification of African sensibilities leads toward the building of an emergent, self-sufficient, rural community by the end of her novel.

About two-thirds through the novel, Celie finds out about her own family history from her sister's letters. With Shug's support, she begins to change, and this change affects all the other characters. After Shug and Celie try unsuccessfully to find the exact grave sites of Celie's parents, Shug tells Celie, "Us each other's peoples now" (167). The final third of the novel is a movement toward a reconciliation of the characters and a reforming of the extended family and community compound. Celie and Shug have come to terms with their own ancestors; furthermore, both have reconnected with their children. The wives and co-wives have come to a sisterly bonding, and even the husbands have shed some of their patriarchal attitudes and become involved members of the family community in a nonhierarchical setting. Harpo and Sophia are reunited, and in what is probably the most utopian of endings, there is even reconciliation between Celie and Albert. When Shug gets involved with a young lover and leaves both Albert and Celie, husband and wife start to find a level of mutual understanding through their love for Shug:

"Here us is, I thought, two old fools left over from love, keeping each other company under the stars" (238). The reconciliation between Celie and Albert is of great import because it not only reflects the possibility of growth in Albert but it also emphasizes the necessity of male-female bonding. In this woman-identified novel, there is still a potent vision of the bonding of the entire Black community. Moreover, as he becomes an elder, Albert gains insight. This concept of age as wisdom—a principle which remains in Africa, but which is lost, for the most part, in mainstream America—strengthens Walker's aim to (re)build the emergent African-American family with the residual qualities of their African heritage.

Another indication that Walker's objective is to recreate a utopian African village community at the end of *The Color Purple* is expressed through her use of clothes making as a cottage industry. Celie's creative sewing turns into a traditional, community enterprise in which all the members of Celie's extended family become engaged. In this way the familial community has become self-sufficient, no longer working for white people as tenant farmers and domestics to survive. The enterprise of making clothes is a communal one, nonhierarchical, and most importantly, it is creative art since the clothes-makers design their clothes in the way that suits them and the wearers best. This freedom of expression is compared to Nettie's description of the clothing styles of the Olinkas, as Celie tells Albert that in Africa, "both men and women preshate a nice dress." And she states more pointedly: "And men sew in Africa, too, I say. / They do? he ast. / Yeah, I say. They not so backwards as mens here" (238). In the spirit of an African tradition, Albert also begins to make clothes; he designs shirts to go with Celie's pants, with big pockets and loose sleeves and no collar—in the style of a dashiki (247).

The final event in the novel is the July Fourth dinner that everyone in the extended family, even Nettie, Samuel, and Celie's children, attends. When asked by Sophia's smallest child why they celebrate on July Fourth, her father, Harpo, answers, "White people busy celebrating they independence from England July 4th . . . so most black folks don't have to work. Us can spend the day celebrating each other" (250). When Nettie arrives with the children, full of "African independence of opinion and outspokenness" (227), the two sisters are reunited, and Celie is finally able to hug her children.

And with one last humorous example of the cultural ties that bind, the family questions Adam's African wife, Tashi: "What your people love best to eat over there in Africa? us ast. / She sort of blush and say *barbecue*" (251).

Celie's last letter is written to God but the God in this letter has been trans/(re)formed to the animist concept of God, perceived not as "that old white man," but as part of nature and oneself, in song and the color purple. She addresses the letter, "Dear God. Dear stars, dear trees, dear sky, dear peoples. Dear everything. Dear God" (249). Walker comments in an interview with John O'Brien, "If there is one thing African-Americans have retained of their African heritage, it is probably animism: a belief that makes it possible to view all creation as living, as being inhabited by spirit" (193). Through this spirit of creation and endurance, the acknowledgment of one's African heritage, the communication with one's ancestors, the acceptance of one's community, and the love of one's sisters, the tragic history of Celie's namesake is transformed, and this triumph can be passed on to the community's children as well as to the reader.

In referring to one of her short stories, "The Revenge of Hannah Kemhuff," Walker foreshadows her experience in writing *The Color Purple*:

> In that story I gathered up the historical and psychological threads of the life my ancestors lived, and in the writing of it I felt joy and strength and my own continuity. I had that wonderful feeling . . . of being *with* a great many people, ancient spirits, all very happy to see me consulting and acknowledging them, and eager to let me know, through the joy of their presence, that, indeed, I am not alone. (*Mothers' Gardens* 13; italics in original)

Returning to Jane Marcus's remark that women's art is a "patient craft," we can see Walker as sewing together the torn strands of her culture's history and making it into herstory. Walker has transformed her great-grandmother's story into a folk novel with a moral, based, to some extent, on the domestic chore of sewing. But Walker's use of this craft may be symbolic as well as literal. According to Walter Ong, "Text, from a root meaning, 'to weave,' is, in absolute terms, more compatible etymologically with oral utterance than is 'literature'. . . . Oral discourse has commonly been thought of even in oral milieus as weaving or stitching" (13). So Walker's use of a cottage industry based on "stitching" may also reflect the oral art from which her text is derived; certainly it is clear that for Walker, as for her African sister-storytellers, art must be usable art—oraliterature that will be told and retold to maintain the health and strength of the community and its children.

# 5

## Toni Morrison, *Song of Solomon*

In *Song of Solomon*, Pilate is the ancestor.

Toni Morrison,
"Rootedness"

■ In recreating an African village compound within the context of the rural South, Alice Walker pays tribute to her African and African-American ancestors. Toni Morrison, in *Song of Solomon*, resonates that ancestry in another way: Morrison tells us that she writes "village literature, fiction that is really for the village, for the tribe" (LeClair 26). Like the tales of the village storytellers, Morrison's writings are deeply entrenched in her own Black folk roots and the community in which she grew up; moreover, her text is informed by her mother's stories, her tribe, and her ancestors, African and African-American. In this chapter, I focus not only on Morrison's use of African values, heritage, characteristics, and community as an alternative to mainstream assimilation or radical separatism, but also on her use of African modes of storytelling and orature as a way of bridging the gap between the Black community's folk roots and the Black American literary tradition.

In the African section of this study, I examined the relationship of African orature to the writers' aims. Their oraliterature is a recursive discourse which (re)members the role of the oral artist—most often the village woman storyteller. This role in a traditional African society is one in which the artist is both participant in and representative of that community. In "Rootedness: The Ancestor as Foundation," Morrison yearns for a closer identification of the Black American artist with her community: "There must have been a time when an artist could be genuinely representative *of* the tribe and *in* it; when an artist could have a tribal or racial sensibility and an individual expression of it" (339). The relationship that Morrison describes is an Afrocentric one, and it is this type of participatory experience that she hopes to recreate in her fiction. My discussion of *Song of Solomon* explores Morrison's role as African storyteller, her use of folklore and the oral tradition, the acceptance of African heritage and culture in modern-day African-American life, the role of the female ancestor, and the generations of women and children who are left to tell the tale. Finally, through Milkman's search, hinged on the verses of a folk song, Morrison can be seen as a trickster who overturns Western biblical and cultural notions through the legends and folkways of her people. From the double entendre of the title to the mythical, contradictory ending, Morrison bears witness to "that civilization that existed underneath the white civilization" (LeClair 26), a society in which the fathers soared and the mothers told stories so that the children would know their names.

*Song of Solomon* is a complex novel which has been seen as a biblical allegory, a detective novel, and a young man's search for his roots. Some male critics, including Mel Watkins of *The New York Times*, have more closely identified with this novel than with Morrison's earlier ones since it is no longer about "the insulated, parochial world of black women," but about Black men (50). As in Aidoo's play, the novel includes a prominent male character, Milkman. Yet the work is equally concerned with the world of Black women (disparaged by Watkins), and the focal character of the novel is Milkman's aunt, Pilate. In a similar manner, mainstream literary critics, more versed in Faulkner than Black folk culture, initially privileged the influence of written discourse on Morrison's writings rather than her oral antecedents no matter how many times she explained her sources.[1] A cursory reading of the novel does not expose it as oraliterature as clearly as a first reading of Walker's *The Color Purple*; the novel is dense, filled with visual description and literary devices. Yet Morrison's role as a storyteller is unmistakable, and as one reads, the orature of her foremothers, as well as the oral traditions of the Black community, is evident in both the language and the structure of the novel. Morrison comments on her own process of recreating the richness of Black speech in her writings: "I have to rewrite, discard, and remove the print-quality of the language to put back the oral quality, where intonation, volume and gesture are all there" (Tate 126). It is Black people's language which is their "grace," Morrison reflects, and what she puts into her fiction, in the manner of the African woman storyteller, is not only the content but the voicings of the stories that were told to her: "When I think of things my mother or father or aunts used to say, it seems the most absolutely striking thing in the world. That is what I try to get into my fiction" (Watkins 48).

Morrison's attention to her writings' oral antecedents extends further than her precise recreation of the voicings of her community or her participatory relationship with the reader. Her works incorporate the use of African and African-American folk tales, folk songs, and legends. In *Sula* (1973), the structure of the novel is based on a legend, a "nigger joke," in which a white farmer gives some rocky hill country to a former slave calling it "the bottom"--the best farming land. *Tar Baby* (1981) is not only based on the famous African-American folk tale, but it also employs the legend of the "Maroons," the escaped slaves with mythical powers. Morrison's novel *Beloved* (1987) transforms historical document to community legend, evoking the voices of "sixty million and more." *Song of Solomon* (1977) is imbued with folk myths and legends from the African diaspora, most importantly, the tale of the Flying Africans— who escape slavery by flying back to Africa. Many legends abound throughout the Americas of Africans who either flew or jumped off slave ships as well as those who saw the horrors of slavery when they landed in the Americas, and "in their anguish, sought to fly back to Africa."[2] For Morrison, as for Paule Marshall (whose Igbos walk back) and Ishmael Reed (whose slave Quickskill flies Air Canada), the notion of using the supernatural, especially this most exalted form of freedom, to overcome a catastrophe captivated her: "I wanted to use black folklore, the magic and superstitious part of it. . . . It's part of our heritage. That's why flying is the central metaphor in Song" (Watkins 50). Clearly, the question of whether the slaves killed themselves or flew back to Africa is culture bound.

From the opening of the novel when insurance agent/Seven Days member Robert Smith either commits suicide or flies away on his own wings, Morrison questions the imposed values and perceptions of the dominant culture and begins to offer alternative cultural knowledge and belief based on Black Americans' African traditions and heritage. Also revealing is the folk song of Sugarman/ Solomon's flying away, sung by Pilate at Milkman's birth. The song is the key to Milkman's quest and illustrates the function of the African-American woman in passing on the stories of her culture's painful yet courageous past. The novel, structured in the manner of a surreal detective story, has a multifaceted plot, but it is Milkman's relationship with his "ancestor" Pilate which transforms his search for gold into an acknowledgment of his heritage. In a quest to learn his family history, Milkman repeats Pilate's journey to Virginia to find her mother's family and ends up uncovering the legend of his ancestors—that of the Flying Africans.

In *Black Feminist Criticism*, Barbara Christian comments that "in dramatizing the traditions of her community, Morrison's novels resemble the oral technique of the storyteller" (57). Equally pertinent to this study is the importance of storytelling within the context of the novel itself: Morrison tells the tale of the Flying Africans to keep her traditions and culture alive on paper; her characters pass on the stories of family and ancestral life, although some "informants" are more reliable than others. In "Recitations to the *Griot*," Joseph Skerrett points out: "Milkman's parents, Macon and Ruth, are not effective informants for Milkman. . . . It is only Pilate for whom storytelling is *not* self-dramatization, self-justification, or egoaction" (194–95). Although Pilate is unmistakably Morrison's preferred storyteller, the other stories and the differing voices further emphasize the oral quality of the novel. For it is the sum of the stories, told by this community of voices in the Midwest, Northeast, and South, and Milkman's ability to select between them, which gives us a greater sense of the workings of the oral tradition. With this sense comes the realization that these tales exist only by the potential in certain human beings to tell them.[3]

Milkman Dead, the recipient of these stories, has an overachieving, dominant, "Black white man," for a father and a beaten-down, faded rose for a mother, and is—at thirty years old—bored. Only his rapport with his father's sister Pilate, a conjurer whose scent is of African ginger, has kept Milkman alive (both literally and metaphorically). Milkman's unravelling of his family history hinges on the decoding of a folk song that Pilate sings at his birth. The words of the song, without specific meaning, have echoed in Milkman's thoughts throughout his young life, and only when he is in Virginia, in the town Shalimar/Solomon, does he realize the original mean-

ing of the song as well as its transition through time and generations. The folk song, carried to her own children by Pilate, is the
story of Milkman's great-grandfather, an enslaved African who es-
capes slavery by flying back to Africa. Only through the retelling of
the tale is this act known, not only to the people of Shalimar, but
also to that African's descendants.

In the dedication of *Song of Solomon*, Morrison writes, "The
fathers may soar / And the children may know their names." But
there is a group missing from the dedication whose presence is
overpowering in the novel itself—the mothers (grandmother, aunt,
older sibling, female ancestor). When the father soars off, there must
be someone left to teach the children their names. Although I discuss the importance of naming and the woman blues of "you can't
fly off a leave a body" later, it is evident that the tales of the Flying
Africans and the stories of endurance and strength in the face of
slavery and oppression, as well as the values of the African communities from whence they came, have been encapsulated in the orature
of the women—left behind not only to sing the blues but to sing of
home. Morrison, in her role as storyteller, creates an environment
within the context of the novel for the stories of women, especially
Pilate's, to be recognized and privileged. Macon's stories direct
Milkman to unrewarding ends; it is Pilate's rendition of their past
which helps Milkman grow.

Morrison's attention to storytelling traditions reflects aspects of
African orature examined in the first part of this study; *Song of
Solomon* also employs African artistic traditions in another way. By
leaving out the "mothers" in her dedication, Morrison has not necessarily forgotten them; rather, it is up to us through our reading of
the book and our own understanding of how women are often left
out of recorded history to fill in what is missing. Morrison comments on the "participatory" quality of her work: "My language has
to have holes and spaces so the reader can come into it. . . . Then we
(you, the reader, and I, the author) come together to make this
book, to feel this experience" (Tate 125). As Morrison's community
of readers, we are constantly called to question values as well as
supply information. Morrison's engagement with her readers (community) appears based on the concept that the "artist in the traditional African milieu spoke for and to his [her] community"
(Chinweizu 241). In the chapter on Aidoo, I note that certain
genres of the orature, particularly the dilemma tales, have unre-

solved endings which call for community response; this is evident in the ending of *Song* as well. Moreover, the participation of the community/audience is often insured by a "chorus" designed to engage them. Like her African sister-storytellers, Morrison also uses this participatory device within the context of written discourse: "To use, even formally, a chorus. The real presence of a chorus. *Meaning the community or the reader at large, commenting on the action as it goes ahead*" ("Rootedness" 341; emphasis added).[4]

One of the questions raised in *Song of Solomon* has plagued Black Americans since emancipation—that of one's place in American society. From DuBois's "double self" to Ralph Ellison's "invisible man," the question of identity in a hostile and antagonistic world has been paramount. Often, this search for identity has led to two opposite approaches: mainstream assimilation/accommodation or radical separatism. Two characters in the novel illustrate these warring factions, Macon Dead, Milkman's father (assimilation) and Guitar Bains, Milkman's friend (separatism). In addition, Milkman's mother, Ruth, appears to symbolize the death of the genteel, bourgeois, light-skin Black who is isolated from her community. Through the characterization of Pilate, Morrison emphasizes the dead-end of both mainstream assimilation and radical separatism by offering an alternative—perhaps not a reconciliation but a more clearly articulated dialectic of the double-self by the acceptance of one's African values and cultural heritage.

African values and African culture, exemplified in Pilate, are privileged in the text. Like the woman in yellow in *Tar Baby*, Pilate has all the qualities Morrison associates with an ideal African woman: She has stature, strength, presence. Pilate is tall, tall as her brother Macon, with black skin and wine-colored lips; moreover, she constantly has a "chewing stick" between her lips, much like a West African market woman. And even if those images are missed by the casual reader, one easily notes Macon's statement to his son, "If you ever have a doubt we from Africa, look at Pilate" (54). Pilate also has mystical powers. She is born without a navel, which allows her special privileges as a conjure woman, even though it separates her—as with any religious figure—from her community. Pilate's house resembles one in an African village compound: she has forgone gas and electricity, using candles and kerosene; she cooks over a three-stone fireplace, and lives "pretty much as though progress was a word that meant walking a little farther down the road" (27). When Milkman and Guitar try to rob Pilate of what they think is the gold, they encounter in the ginger-smelling air a surreal middle passage back to the West African coast from whence their ancestors were stolen:

> Breathing the air that could have come straight from a marketplace in Accra, they stood for what seemed to them a very long time. Although they had stood deliberately in the dark of the pine trees, they were unprepared for the deeper darkness that met them there in that room. Neither had seen that kind of blackness, not even behind their own eyes. (186)

Pilate's house reflects her African heritage in other ways. Her house appears to her in-law Ruth as "an inn, a safe harbor" (135), and "true to the palm oil that flowed in her veins," Pilate offers both food and hospitality to any who enter (150). Even Macon, who deserted his sister, sees the house as a place of music, warmth, and caring, not realizing that he has destroyed the music in his own house. The two houses stand in stark contrast. In the Deads' house, built by Ruth's acerbic and bourgeois father, the women cower and Milkman is bored. Ruth suffers under Macon's rule, her creativity stunted, her flowers dying. The two daughters, Magdalene called Lena and First Corinthians, pine for lack of love and life, since no man in the community is good enough for Macon Dead's daughters. In contrast to this "dead" house, the women in Pilate's house can live and breathe and sing, three generations worth, in harmony (28). There is deep familial bonding between grandmother Pilate, mother Reba, and daughter Hagar. The grandmother, as mentioned earlier, has had a profound influence on the socialization of children in both African and African-American cultures, and Pilate is certainly the head of this household. Ironically, it is Milkman, brought into existence through Pilate's powers, who practically destroys the foundation of these women's lives.

This irony is even more pointed since Milkman is Pilate's chosen recipient of the knowledge of their family heritage. Furthermore, it is intriguing that Morrison chooses a son to make the search rather than any of the daughters in the novel. Perhaps it is because Morrison herself has two sons and hoped to examine the "leaving home" of Black men beyond the sociological notion of the absent father (Stepto 486–87). This choice may also illustrate the dominant role the female ancestor/mother plays in passing on cultural knowledge and values to both male and female children in the family. In this case, Pilate reflects West African practices, examined in the chapter on Nwapa, where the education of the children—until the boys' initiation—is the responsibility of the women of the familial compound. Pilate seems to understand the necessity of Milkman's life before he is born. Returning to find her brother a "hard man" and her sister-in-law dying from lack of love, she gives Ruth a greenish-grey powder to put in Macon's food so as to revive their sex lives (131). When Pilate finds out later that Macon is trying to abort the child conceived in deception, she reminds him of her obeah powers: She puts a male doll with a chicken bone stuck between its legs in his office (132). Pilate is what Morrison calls the "black woman as parent"; she is a community parent, "a sort of umbrella figure, a culture bearer" (Stepto 488).

As a culture bearer in touch with her ancestry, Pilate holds conversations with her dead father; moreover, she has an uncanny knowledge of events she has not witnessed. She knows her mother's history and the colors of her mother's ribbons even though her mother died with her birth. Moreover, after Milkman and Guitar steal the bones they believe to be gold, Pilate goes to the police station and weaves a "sambo" story to save them, incorporating information which she could not possibly have learned in any rational way. Later, Macon remarks to Milkman: "Who knows what Pilate knows?" (207). To get her bag of bones back, Pilate takes on the changeable characteristics of Legba. Legba, the African deity worshipped throughout the Caribbean, is discussed more fully in the next chapter. Almost as tall as Macon, she shrinks herself in front of the police, turning her strong powerful African presence into a stereotypic imitation of Aunt Jemima (208).

Pilate is omnipresent in the novel, and many of her values and powers are passed on to her daughter and granddaughter. Reba, for example, wins every contest she enters in spite of the fact that she has no interest in the prizes. The image of the three generations of women living in harmony, plaiting hair and singing songs mirrors Efuru's village compound, yet the constraints of being Black in America shatter this image. For all her powers, Pilate is unable to bring her extended family back together as a force to confront racial oppression, nor is she able to save Hagar from the imposition of the white dominant culture's definition of beauty after Hagar and Milkman's incestuous relationship ends in disaster.

Exogamy, in most African societies, insures that the children from an upcoming marriage will be healthy, productive members of society. As illustrated in the African section of this study, it is one of the most important considerations in mate selection. According to sociologist Kamene Okonjo, exogamy helps justify the involvement of the extended family in that selection, since the elders would know who was a relative ("Aspects of Continuity and Change" 8). The sexual relationship between Milkman and his cousin Hagar is doomed at the start since it breaks this African cultural practice. In many West African languages, terms like "cousin," "nephew," and "niece" do not exist. Pilate foreshadows the disastrous end to their relationship by referring to Milkman as Hagar's brother rather than cousin. When both Reba and Hagar correct her, Pilate questions the difference between the two words: "I mean what's the difference in the way you act towards 'em? . . . Then why they got two words for it 'stead of one, if they ain't no difference?" (44).

Another African practice, prolonged (in Western terms) breast-feeding, functions antithetically in the novel. It is a source of embarrassment for both Milkman and Macon and shows the intense loneliness and apparent uselessness of Ruth. Moreover, it is how Milkman gets his name. But Milkman's prolonged breast-feeding also highlights the conflict of values in the novel. When the yardman Freddie witnesses one of Milkman's afternoon suckings, his comments reflect both the knowledge of this traditional practice and the dominant culture's view that the experience is somehow obscene: "I be damn, Miss Rufie. . . . I don't even know the last time I seen that. I mean, ain't nothing wrong with it. I mean, old folks swear by it" (14). Freddie's renaming of Milkman represents a major occurrence in Milkman's life and becomes family history. Melville Herskovits, in *The Myth of the Negro Past*, focuses on the importance of naming in African-American culture. He associates these naming practices with those of their African forebears and comments:

> Names are of great importance in West Africa. . . . That is why, among Africans, a person's name may in so many instances change

with time, a new designation being assumed on the occasion of
some striking occurrence in his life, or when he goes through one of
the rites marking a new stage in his development. (191)

The importance of names and naming in the novel could be the
subject of a study itself, but naming as a method of resisting the
hegemony of white society through African cultural practices is of
primary concern here. The power of a name is so strong in Africa
and the diaspora that often people kept a secret name so that an
enemy could not use it for evil intent; moreover, a name could also
be employed as a counterhegemonic response to one's oppressor, as
slaves (who retained African names or signified in a secret language)
were wont to do.[5] The biblical names used in the novel signify
"secret" names since they rarely fit the person named (Pilate, of
course, is the most obvious example). Morrison comments: "I used
the biblical names to show the impact of the Bible on the lives of
Black people, their awe and respect for it coupled with their ability *to
distort it for their own purposes*" (LeClair 28; emphasis added). From
Sing Dead's insistence that her husband, Jake, should keep the misguided name he was given by an illiterate white man and Pilate's
wearing of her name in her ear to the constant process of oppositional naming and renaming that occurs in the novel, it is evident
that naming is a method of regaining control of one's life. Moreover, this process demonstrates the pattern of passing on the unique
cultural traits of Africa within the context of the African-American
community. I would further suggest that, in response to Morrison's
dedication, it may not be necessary to learn one's original African
name—it is the process of naming which must survive.

Explicit aspects of African cultural heritage in *Song* are the supernatural occurrences throughout the novel. They attest to the alternative reality presented in Morrison's cultural discourse. The acceptance of the supernatural is treated, for the most part, very differently
in African and Western cultures. Rather than the Anglo-American
modernist view of literature as one's relationship to one's "id," Wole
Soyinka, in *Myth, Literature and the African World View*, describes
African literature as one's relationship to the cosmos, rational and
irrational. Morrison emphasizes that aspect of Black Americans' African heritage in comments about *Song*:

[With that novel], I could blend the acceptance of the supernatural and a profound rootedness in the real world at the same time with neither taking precedence over the other. It is indicative of the cosmology, the way in which Black people looked at the world. . . . And some of those things were "discredited knowledge" that Black people had; discredited only because Black people were discredited therefore what they *knew* was "discredited." . . . That knowledge has a very strong place in my work. ("Rootedness" 342)

It is this special, discredited knowledge that Pilate has. Macon tells Milkman to stay away from Pilate because she is a "snake" and explains the way of the world to him in hard-core materialist terms: "After school come to my office; work a couple of hours there and learn what's real. Pilate can't teach you a thing you can use in this world. *Maybe the next, but not this one*" (55; emphasis added). Macon makes a sharp division between the material and spiritual world, privileging the material, but there are other characters, deeply rooted in the African-American tradition, who have a more integrated world view. These people, mostly women, extend their knowledge of African-American life to include an African perspective in which there is dialogue with the ancestors, extended longevity, and perceptions of "things" outside a narrow, literalist vision. Paul Carter Harrison points out that this is not surrealism within a modernist context: "Dialogue between living and dead members of the community should not be misconstrued as surrealism: What is important to the mode here is simply the materialization of the ancestral spirit so that one is able to identify the precise source of a particular piece of wisdom" (19). Therefore, the presence of ancestor (alive or dead) and the wisdom one receives from that source is seen within the context of the African continuum.

Both of Milkman's "mothers" (Ruth and Pilate) speak with their dead fathers. Ruth, who was "pressed small" by a society which would not allow her to grow, believed her father to be the only friend that she had (124). Unfortunately, her father, isolated from his own community, added to Ruth's "smallness" and alienation so that her love for him has become distorted with profanity. Still her trips to his grave to "speak" with him reflect the ongoing continuum from the ancestors to the descendants. Pilate's relationship with her dead father is clearly more sustaining than Ruth's. Unlike

Ruth's father, Jake (the first Macon Dead) is a proud and connected member of his community. Before his murder, he was a successful farmer, but he did not set himself apart from others in the community; moreover, in death, he still directs Pilate and helps her to understand her life and heritage. She explains to Ruth: "It's a good feeling to know he's around. I tell you he's a person I can always rely on" (141). Through the words and actions of her father and the prenatal knowledge she gains from her mother, Pilate begins to unravel the family history, which she passes on to the next generation through Milkman.

Another influential character whose very presence bespeaks the supernatural quality of the novel is Circe, the servant who saves Macon and Pilate after their father dies. She is professed to be almost one hundred years old when she hides the two children in the house of the white people who murdered their father, and she seems twice that old when Milkman, close to fifty years later, meets her in his search for the gold. She is the last remaining human in the old mansion, and like Uncle Robin in *Flight to Canada*, she has outlived her oppressors. Milkman's ability to accept Circe in spite of obvious contradictions of her existence illustrates his acknowledgment of this aspect of his heritage. Furthermore, his meeting with Circe and his trip to the cave start to alter the object of his search from the gold to his roots. Milkman is comfortable with waking dreams, ghosts, and supernatural occurrences, for he states: "Pilate did not have a navel. Since that was true, anything could be, and why not ghosts as well?" (298). It is this ability which separates him from the stark materialism of his father and allows him to understand and respect Pilate's powers. And although it takes him almost twenty years to truly comprehend the importance of what she says, his initial meeting with Pilate and her daughters had been "the first time in his life that he remembered being completely happy" (47).

The relationship between Pilate and Milkman is the focal one of the novel, and the beginning of this relationship reveals further evidence of the supernatural as part of Morrison's cultural discourse. As noted earlier, Pilate prepares a potion for Macon so that he will sleep with his wife. But Pilate is not only thinking of solving the loneliness of Ruth; she is also worried that the family males may end with the alienated Macon. Pilate's interest in the continuation of her family is typical of most human yearnings, but in another way Pilate seems to prophesy Milkman's coming not only as a repository for the family's history but also as a reincarnation of Milkman's great-grandfather Solomon, the Flying African. The importance of this theme is reflected in Morrison's change of title from her earlier "Milkman Dead" to the published *Song*. Pilate's statement to Ruth that Macon should have a son might appear idle guessing (125), but since Pilate's powers are well documented, it seems as if she willed Milkman to come or at least acted as the liaison between the ancestors and the unborn. Morrison returns to this theme in *Beloved*. Throat slashed by her fugitive slave mother, Beloved is "reincarnated" as a young woman who reenters her mother's post-slavery life.

Reincarnation, as it functions in the diaspora, remains a powerful concept within an African world view. African scholar Donatus Nwoga comments that although this concept, as "rationally valid acceptable knowledge," is yet to be explored, both traditional religion and contemporary literature explores reincarnation in the Black world.[6] By the end of the novel, Milkman's flight, which mirrors his great-grandfather's, seems predestined. Milkman, who is born under the blue satin wings of Robert Smith's suicide/flight, is imprinted with the desire to fly: "Mr. Smith's blue silk wings must have left their mark, because when the little boy discovered, at four, the same thing that Mr. Smith had learned earlier—that only birds and airplanes could fly—he lost all interest in himself" (9). Morrison gives us the flight of Robert Smith as the reason Milkman wants so desperately to fly, but since Morrison misleads us so many times in the course of this "dilemma tale," there is reason to suspect this statement may be another example. By the end of the novel, Milkman's yearning for flight seems intricately connected with the history of the great-grandfather; if indeed he is the reincarnation of this African, the desire to fly would have been there whether he felt the prenatal flapping of his mother's stomach or not. I am not suggesting that Robert Smith, the insurance agent who may also have been flying to escape his form of slavery, is not at all connected with Milkman's propensity for flight nor the alternative reality of the novel; rather Smith's take-off from Mercy Hospital appears to echo the flight of Solomon and this collective myth of freedom throughout the diaspora.

Milkman's penchant for flight is what leads him to seek the gold his father wants retrieved. Macon sends his son because he still thinks the gold is in the cave in which Pilate and he hid after their father was killed. Clearly, Milkman's own search is not directed solely toward finding the gold as it is for both his father and Guitar. On the airplane, he feels freed from his world where "the wings of all those other people's nightmares flapped in his face and constrained him" (222). Milkman envisions this trip back east as an escape from the drudgery of his life, but through the instructions of Pilate, the search for gold becomes a greater search for family history and African heritage. Milkman's search takes him further than his grandfather's farm in Pennsylvania; he returns to the world the slaves made—the South.

The American South, in spite of its iniquitous history of racial segregation and slavery, has become for many African-American writers a source of heritage, one's familial home. This may seem, and perhaps is, ironic but the fact remains that this is where Afro-America began and where the relationship to one's African roots is the strongest. From Harrison's *The Great MacDaddy*, in which the protagonist travels from Los Angeles to the Sea Islands in South Carolina to find the "source," to contemporary women writers such as Toni Cade Bambara, Gloria Naylor, and Paule Marshall, movement south reaffirms a connection to the African diaspora. Morrison is no exception, and Milkman's trip south—this time to Virginia— finally leads him to an understanding of himself, his family, and his culture. Milkman's growing comprehension that rural life differs dramatically from the life he has known in the city starts when he visits his grandfather's community in Pennsylvania. As he hears stories about his family heritage, he realizes a strength in his culture that he had paid little attention to in the past: He realizes that the word "people" meant "links" (231). Milkman's appreciation that people may be more important than material goods, that family and community is a strength, and that knowing your heritage is a power separate from the power of money starts to affect him in both conscious and subconscious ways. To search for the gold surreptitiously, Milkman makes up a story that he is going to look for his grandfather's remains (251). Yet it is the search for his ancestors, not necessarily for the remains but for the remainder of the story, that directs Milkman to Virginia. He follows not the gold of his father but the song and story of his aunt: "Macon didn't even try to get to Virginia. Pilate headed straight for it" (297).

Milkman's journey south is a learning experience for him as he pieces together the different stories and lore of his family. But there are other aspects of the South and his culture of which he, from an isolated, assimilated family, has only glimpsed in the presence of his aunt. He notices that the women do not carry purses and that their walk and carriage reflect a proud heritage that the overly made-up city women have lost. The women remind him of Pilate: "Wide sleepy eyes that tilted up at the corners, high cheekbones, full lips blacker than their skin, berry-stained, and long, long necks" (266). In addition to the slow pace and sense of community that he finds in Shalimar (pronounced Shallimone/Solomon—another renaming), he realizes that he is unlearned in rural customs. He alienates the men around him by his garish display of wealth, and before they accept him, he has to go through an initiation consisting of hunting and fighting. Moreover, he has to reconnect with the natural world before he can clearly see what is right in front of him. Pertinently, Milkman's awareness of the community around him leads him to reassess his family and their values as well as his own selfishness. He sees his extended family in a different light and is sympathetic to both his father's distorted ambition and his mother's pathetic help-lessness. His thoughts encompass both those he hurt and ignored and those who were out to "kill" him; however, they center on his two "mothers," who never wanted to take his life, but had given it to him—one physically, the other spiritually (335).

In the epigraph to this chapter, Morrison states that Pilate func-tions as the ancestor in *Song*, and it is under her guidance that Milkman becomes responsible and humane; moreover, it is her stor-ies and songs passed on to all of her children which not only lead him to unravel his family history but implant in him the desire to know. Pilate's most important role is her position as village woman storyteller, the primary one in the family to pass on the tales of the ancestors to the children. And although she cannot save her own granddaughter from the imposing environment that inevitably de-stroys Hagar, she manages to protect both Ruth and Milkman, and in the end she gives Milkman not only his birthright but a legacy which allows him, too, to fly: "She had told him stories, sang him songs . . . and on the first cold day of the year, [fed him] hot nut soup" (211). More than the traditional West African dish fed to him, Pilate gives Milkman back his heritage through her African-based orature, although it takes him years to understand the true value of the tales and songs. Most significantly, the children's song, turned into a women's blues by Pilate, is what leads Milkman to the legacy of his great-grandfather and the Flying Africans.

From the homophone of Pilate's name to Robert Smith's flying on his own wings and the Shalimar children's rendition of the folk song with the sounds of an airplane, the desire to fly and its execution, much discussed by critics, is a major motif in *Song*. This motif markedly augments the alternate reality of an African world view presented here. The song from Pilate's voice that accompanies Milkman's birth and which he hears throughout his life helps Milkman to realize that he is descended from the Flying Africans who refused to exist under the confines and humiliation of slavery. As Milkman listens to the ancient words of the song sung by children who do not even understand the African words like "yaruba" (possibly Yoruba), he begins to piece together his family history as told to him by Pilate, Circe, and his grandmother Sing's niece, Susan Byrd, a Native American. Byrd (her name a further configuration of the flying motif) not only confirms Milkman's thoughts about the song but tells him about the flying. Milkman asks her incredulously, "Why did you call Solomon a flying African?" She answers: "A lot of them flew back to Africa. The one around here who did was this same Solomon" (326). When Milkman returns to his lover Sweet, with whom sex is also a dream of flying (302), he is vibrant as he tells her what he always felt but never knew—that somewhere in his ancestry, someone could fly: "No more cotton! No more bales! No more orders! No more shit! He flew, baby. Lifted his beautiful black ass up in the sky and flew on home" (332).

The reader's enjoyment at Milkman's elation is marred by the account of Hagar's death (chapter 13), sandwiched in between the two chapters on Milkman's comprehension and acceptance of his birthright. Evidently, Morrison is quick to remind us that the one flying away leaves people behind, most often the women and their children. Neither Solomon's wife, Ryna, nor Hagar can function after being left, and both basically die of broken hearts. Hagar unfortunately has inherited the weakness of her great-great-grandmother and does not really hear the stories told to her by Pilate. These traits are further exacerbated by the imposition of the dominant culture, the lack of a truly extended family, and Milkman's selfishness. But there is another female tradition encoded in the myth of the Flying Africans—the tradition of women left to tell the tale; these are the ones who pass on the stories so that the children will know their names. In the context of this tradition, Morrison states: "There is a price to pay and the price is the children. . . . All the men have left someone, and it is the children who remember it, sing about it, make it a part of their family history" (Watkins 50). It is the women who have kept track of the names and stories so that the men could soar and the children could learn and remember. Pilate hears the words from her father, "You just can't fly off and leave a body," and she lives her life that way—a lament for those who left and a commitment, from the bones of her father to the name that is pierced in her ear, to bear witness. Pilate tells the tale the young ones would not even have guessed without her. Indeed, the men who fly off have a price to pay for disappearing without a thought to the women and children left behind; however, Morrison seems to say that not all women are destroyed by an oppressive system's dissolution of their family (for the men would not have had to fly away if they were not subject to slavery). Just as spirituals transformed the slaves' misery into music, Pilate and the other women storytellers turn their "plea into a note" (321) and pass on the memory of the names that were stolen and the stories suppressed.

Apropos to this transformational aspect of the storytelling which uncovers the words hidden by the dominant culture is Morrison's statement: "If you come from Africa, your name is gone. It is particularly problematic because it is not just *your* name but your family, your tribe. When you die how can you connect with your ancestors if you have lost your name?" (LeClair 28). The concept of knowing one's name, tribe, and cultural heritage is paramount to the novel, but Morrison goes one step further; she shows the necessity of stripping off the layers of dominant culture which has hidden both the names and values of "that civilization which exists underneath." In the manner of a trickster tale teller, Morrison leads the reader in the prescribed direction only to pull the rug. Most readers even vaguely familiar with the Bible will immediately assume the title of the novel relates in some way to the Old Testament's love song, but as the plot unravels, the song is that of the Flying African Solomon. As in earlier examples of the use of naming, Morrison emphasizes the ability of Black people to subvert images of dominant white Christian values to expose underlying cosmologies while taking on some of the characteristics of the original.

Not only does Morrison use the trickster tale to demonstrate the ability Black people have to turn around the mythologies of the West, she ends her novel in the manner of an African dilemma tale. In *Dilemma of a Ghost*, Aidoo uses this form of the orature to underscore the conflict of the Western-educated African; Morrison's participatory ending compels us to focus on another conflict—the hegemonic Western notion that science is the sole explanation of the universe. The end of *Song of Solomon* has evoked much critical discussion on what happens to Milkman at Solomon's Leap. After he witnesses Pilate's murder by Guitar, Milkman offers his life to his friend and leaps: "As fleet and bright as a lodestar, he wheeled toward Guitar and it did not matter which one of them would give up his ghost in the killing arms of his brother. For now he knew what Shalimar knew: If you surrendered to the air, you could *ride* it" (341). One question which has been raised is whether Milkman lives or dies. Reynolds Price, in a *New York Times* review, asks, "Does Milkman survive to use his new knowledge, or does he die at the hands of a hateful friend?" (48). The ending of the novel is unresolved, but I am assured that the question the reader should ponder in this dilemma tale is not whether Milkman lives or dies; rather, the question is whether Milkman dies or flies! Which perception of reality are we to believe?

As evidenced by slavers' reports, many slaves committed suicide by jumping overboard during the Middle Passage. Yet the mythology of African-American and Caribbean peoples tells us that the slaves flew back to Africa. If Morrison is ending this novel in the style of an African dilemma tale, there is both a question and a caveat for the reader: In a multicultural society, there may be other perceptions of reality, other values, and other ways of interpretation than the ones ordained by the dominant culture. In this case, Morrison exposes the conflict of Western and African cultural perceptions, revealing the importance of one's African heritage and values for Black Americans. In the reincarnation of his great-grandfather, and through the instructions of his ancestor and aunt, Milkman flies as his ancestors flew, leaving a legacy for women's tales and children's songs.

# 6

## Paule Marshall,
## *Praisesong for the Widow*

[The ancestor figure is] who made my being
possible, and whose spirit continues to ani-
mate my life and work. . . . I am, in a word,
an unabashed ancestor worshipper.

Paule Marshall,
"To Da-duh"

■ In "Rootedness," Toni Morrison comments on the
presence of an ancestor in contemporary Black literature as well as in
her own writings. Marshall's statement above attests to the way her
life and work have been informed by the presence of ancestors, both
"African and New World" (95). In this tribute to her grandmother
Da-duh, Marshall places herself within a continuum from her African foremothers to the present through the guiding hand of this
female ancestor. She further notes that in all of her novels, at least
one elderly woman functions as the ancestor for the main protagonist in the manner of Da-duh. Da-duh appears as the old hairdresser,
Mrs. Thompson, in *Brown Girl, Brownstones* (1959), as the healer
and protector Leesy and cook Carrington in her second novel, *The
Chosen Place, the Timeless People* (1969), and as Avey's Great-aunt
Cuney in *Praisesong for the Widow* (1983). This chapter focuses on
Marshall's novel *Praisesong for the Widow* and emphasizes the role of
the ancestor in maintaining generational and cultural continuity as
part of African-American/Caribbean life. *Praisesong* is a consonant
end to this study since it explores the dialectics of reconciliation, a

coming-to-terms with both the African and the American aspects of the Black American experience. I focus on Marshall's role as storyteller and her debt to the orature of her foremothers, the conflict of values in Black American middle-class life, the understanding of one's heritage by a middle passage back through the Caribbean, and the articulation of the African/American self through the guidance of the ancestors.

Marshall's novels make manifest the view that a return to an African consciousness is more clearly visualized in the Caribbean where, she feels, stronger ties to one's ancestors have remained. Her own parents emigrated to the United States from Barbados, and as a child of Afro-Caribbean parents, she was brought up with a diaspora consciousness. On her trips back to the Caribbean to visit her grandmother Da-duh as well as for her own research, Marshall has identified this world as a step closer to their African past. She relates this learning process, developed in the discourse of her text, to the "Great Circuit" of slave trading which connected North America and the Caribbean with Africa: "Taken together, the three books . . . constitute a trilogy describing, in reverse, the slave trade's triangular route back to the motherland, the source" ("Shaping the World" 107). In each of her novels, her main female character takes a spiritual "Middle Passage back" to rediscover as well as pass on the history and stories of her people,[1] whether it be Selina's trip to the Caribbean at the end of *Brown Girl, Brownstones,* Merle's voyage to Africa in *The Chosen Place,* or Avey's jumping ship and finding herself in the Caribbean in *Praisesong.*

Marshall, like the other authors in this section, underscores the essentiality of acknowledging one's African heritage for an integrated African-American life, especially for relatively successful, assimilated middle-class Blacks. Moreover, the search for one's heritage—in this case, to remember one's tribe and legend—is seen as a woman's search. In the novel, telling the tales which must be passed on from generation to generation to maintain cultural continuity and wholeness is the function of the women, both the female characters and Marshall herself. When asked which writers influenced her writings, Marshall looks first to the oral artists who passed on their stories to her. She cites her female ancestors, particularly her mother and mother's friends, those poets in the kitchen, as the primary influence on her life and work:

They taught me my first lessons in narrative art. They trained my ear. They set a standard of excellence. That is why the best of my work must be attributed to them: *it stands a test to the rich legacy of language and culture they so freely passed on to me in the wordshop of the kitchen.* ("From the Poets in the Kitchen" 11–12; emphasis added)

In this essay, Marshall details the influence of these women and the orature of her African/Caribbean heritage on her oraliterature—in subject, structure, and language. She emphasizes, as does Walker, that for their foremothers the oral tradition and the powerful use of language was the "only vehicle readily available to them" to express their creative energies. They "made of it an art form that—in keeping with the African tradition in which art and life are one—was an integral part of their lives" ("From the Poets" 6). Marshall explains the strength and solace that these women received from their oral art as they transformed the language—standard English from the Barbadian schools and the African syntax and intonation that survived—and reformed the stories from the rich legacy of their cultural heritage. Impressed by the way the kitchen-poets mastered the ancient art of storytelling, passed down from the "old women [who told stories] to the children seated outside the round houses," Marshall states: "They didn't know it, nor did I at the time, but they were carrying on a tradition as ancient as Africa, centuries old oral mode by which the culture and history, the wisdom of the race had been transmitted" ("Shaping the World" 103). In the African-American section of this study, I have emphasized the women writers' use of African modes of artistic production as recursive discourse. Clearly, Marshall exposes the retention of the orature as an integral part of the kitchen-poets' lives, passed down from their African foremothers. Moreover, she interweaves the remembered sounds as part of her cultural text. From the plangent, mellifluous sounds of Marshall's language read aloud, it is evident that she brings to her writings this ancient African art of storytelling, but more than that, the stories themselves mirror the tradition of telling tales as a means of sustaining social values as they are passed on from generation to generation.[2]

The storytelling tradition in Marshall's work is primarily a woman's domain. As noted earlier, African women's traditional role in the community is that of child socialization and the passing on of the values and traditions. Since this education has often been accomplished by stories and songs commemorating the lives and the legends, both African and African-American women have used their creative energy to "remember the past so as to transform it and make it usable" (Washington, "Afterword" 319). Marshall, in the manner of her female ancestors, pays attention to generational and cultural continuity through the stories and legends of her "tribe," and her main female characters learn of their heritage most often from other women. Each of her three novels centers on certain characters' ability to remember and retell so that future generations as well as the reader will know. Selina, the young woman in *Brown Girl, Brownstones,* reminds us of a young Marshall, a griot of family history, a storyteller who learns from her family and community and, by the end of the novel, travels to Barbados to recover the rest of the stories. *The Chosen Place, the Timeless People* is a more complex novel than the earlier one, but it is also informed by the stories of the ancestors and imbued with Afro-Caribbean legends, such as the tale of Cuffy Ned. *Praisesong for the Widow,* the subject of this chapter, prepares us for immersion into African and African-American orature by the use of the traditional African praisesong in its title. The novel in which Avey Johnson recovers her heritage and accepts her mission to pass it on to the children is indeed a praisesong to this widow: Avey not only learns to sing the praises of the ancestors but she, too, is remembered.

As in *Song of Solomon,* the central myth/legend of *Praisesong for the Widow* is that of the Africans who escaped slavery through supernatural powers. In this novel, the folk tale is not about "flying" Africans but rather about the Igbos at "Ibo Landing" who walked on water and walked on back to Africa.[3] This variant of the Flying African tale surfaces in *Black Folktales* by Julius Lester (148) and Alex Haley's *Roots* (326). But whether the Africans walked or flew, the tale has been passed down through generations with a similar meaning—freedom from oppression and the passage back to Africa. In conversation Marshall told me that, for *Praisesong,* she drew upon a version of the legend in a 1940s WPA project, *Drums and Shadows.* The Igbos, as recounted by a slave who saw them land, all started singing and marched first to the ocean and then across it, although the speaker (from a Western perspective) tells us that they never made it back to Africa—they drowned. Marshall commented that her reading of the legend so resonated in her consciousness that she knew a novel would come out of it. In the resulting *Praisesong*, Marshall takes one step further in accepting the literal meaning of the tale. The ancestor, Great-aunt Cuney, tells the young Avey what Cuney's own grandmother saw when the Ibos disembarked at Ibo Landing. Clearly, the Ibos didn't like what they saw, but as Cuney's gran' tells, they were horrified by what they *foresaw* as the future of the enslaved Africans. So as a collective group, they moved toward the edge of the river and decided to walk back to Africa: "Those Ibos! Just upped and walked away not two minutes after getting here" (39). One time, Sunday-school educated Avey thinks to ask why they didn't drown. Cuney responds: "Did it say Jesus drowned when he went walking on the water in that Sunday school book your momma always sends with you?" (40). As far as Cuney is concerned, the legend of the Africans who walked back to Africa is no less believable than Christ's miracle at the Sea of Galilee; through Aunt Cuney's impeccable logic, Marshall reminds us that certain legends are privileged while others are not. By the retelling of this tale, Marshall brings to the reader an important African-American legend as well as focuses on the necessity of valuing the nonwestern traditions of the Americas—in this case, those of African origin.

The legend of the Africans, which is passed on to Avey by her Great-aunt Cuney and Cuney's gran' is part of an orature which affirms strength and positive action in the midst of oppression. According to Keith Sandiford, the Ibos' refusal to accept Western limitations of time and technology "effectively inaugurated for their Tatem heirs a historical agenda of resistance, denial, and affirmation" (377). As documented in the chapter on Morrison, the power of this tale has resonated throughout the African diaspora, and its retelling strengthens the connections between Black people in the Americas. Marshall, whose cultural heritage is both African-American and Caribbean, has observed from personal experience the cultural continuity of the two areas. In her first and third novels, the Caribbean is a stepping stone to the acknowledgment of one's African heritage; each character's spiritual middle passage back begins with the West Indies.

For Avey Johnson, the protagonist in *Praisesong*, her spiritual middle passage back to Africa begins in an ironically mainstream American leisure activity—a Caribbean cruise. Avey and two friends spend their vacations partaking of the "good life"; this year it is the sun and sea of the tourist-pamphlet West Indies. But as the novel opens, Avey is disconcerted in this environment and decides to return to her "safe" home in White Plains. Fortunately for Avey's spiritual growth, travel is not always convenient in the Caribbean islands, and she is unable to get a plane home until the next day. Avey's stay over in Grenada becomes an excursion to one of the out-islands, Carriacou, and this excursion becomes a voyage back to her African past. With the help of the elderly women on the boat, the androgynous Lebert Joseph, and the memory of her Aunt Cuney's recitations, Avey comes to accept her own cultural heritage, hidden for years by the imposition of the dominant culture and the ironic pressure to assimilate into a restrictive society.

Avey does not tell her two friends why she is leaving the cruise, but she lets the reader know: Her decision stems from two apparently unconnected occurrences—her inability to eat a deliciously rich parfait and the dream she has had about her Great-aunt Cuney. The parfait reflects all the overabundance on the cruise, leaving her with a "vague bloated feeling" like a "huge tumor" (52). But the physical reaction to the overrich food is symptomatic of Avey's spiritual malaise, and she becomes unable to separate her nightmare from reality. In Avey's disturbed vision, the white faces on the cruise become images of skeletons, and the shot skeet becomes a wounded, dying bird (54; 56). As Avey makes the important decision to leave the ship, her friend Thomasina angrily predicts the profound nature of Avey's choice in a threatening statement: "A person would have to have a reason for doing a thing like this. No, somethin's deep behind this mess" (25).

What is "deep behind this mess" becomes evident in the dream-text which bursts from Avey's unconscious before she leaves the cruise. In her dream, Aunt Cuney appears before Avey at Ibo Landing in Tatem, South Carolina. She mutely begs Avey to come with her to enact the ritual of their communal heritage. As Cuney's pleading turns into a demand, the two women struggle: "The fight raged on. . . . With the fur stole like her hard-won life of the past thirty years being trampled into the dirt underfoot" (45). The stole, symbolic of Avey's materialistic, middle-class existence, is pitched against her spiritual needs in the battle. When Avey awakes, she still feels the force of Cuney's hand twisting her wrist. Refusing to analyze her dream, she is aware only of being bothered by something she cannot name (25).

The stole versus the story is representative of a conflict of values that has informed every chapter of this study—the material values of the dominant culture in contradistinction to the spiritual values of the oppressed group. I am not suggesting that the author's view is that one has to forgo material possessions to accept one's cultural heritage, but rather that the societal restraints and the imposition of the dominant culture demand a denial of ethnic identity to succeed. Joyce Pettis notes that the "problems between American middle-class economic status and the retention of cultural values important to African-Americans" are evident in Marshall's fiction (12). For *Praisesong*'s Avey and Jay Johnson, the dialectical tension of this conflict is symbolized by Halsey Street and the "cycle of poverty." In a hotel in Grenada, Avey's memories return to her Brooklyn tenement. Her first thoughts of Halsey Street are positive ones. She remembers the rituals which revolved around the jazz, the blues, and the poems of Black American life. The music and the dreams, not yet deferred, brought sustenance to Avey and Jay's young marriage, and their rich sexual life was informed by African female deities—Yemoja, Oya—and Haitian Erzulie Frieda (127). But Avey's warm thoughts are soon clouded by the reality of what Halsey Street was: the poverty, the hunger, the despair. Although Jay manages to overcome the odds and improve his family's lives economically, it is clear that a price has been exacted for the improvement. The family no longer has time for the rituals and stories of their heritage; the children are solemn; and the trips to Tatem are cancelled. In Avey's mind, Jay has become "Jerome Johnson," who builds up their lives materially but has lost the spiritual quality. Still, Avey does not blame this transformation on Jay alone, but on the oppressive society which demands one's identity as a price for success. On the balcony of the hotel, as Avey thinks back to this change in Jay, she envisions herself as a "Dahomey woman warrior" who wants to battle the dominant culture for her husband's life and bring back the Jay who died with the birth of the upwardly mobile Jerome.

The transition of Jay into Jerome Johnson illustrates what is destroyed in denial and assimilation as well as the emphasis on economic advancement at all costs. Avey perceives her warm reminiscences of Halsey Street as an act of betrayal to Jay, since he remembered not the positive aspects but the fear and poverty: "Like someone unable to recover from a childhood trauma . . . , Jerome

Johnson never got over Halsey Street" (88). Like Macon Dead, he begins to incorporate the prejudices of the dominant culture and looks at the poorer members of his community disdainfully (131). At Jay's funeral, Avey sees a face superimposed on Jay's which she had only glimpsed before, a thin-lipped, pallid, joyless face—the face of a white man—which has finally taken complete control of Jay in death. In her acknowledgment of her own part in denying her heritage, she evaluates their lives:

> Dimly, through the fog of her grief, Avey Johnson understood something vivid and affirming and charged with feeling had been present in those small rituals that had once shaped their lives. . . . Something in those small rites, an ethos they held in common, had reached back beyond her life and beyond Jay's to join them to the vast unknown lineage that made their being possible. (137)

In her tourist hotel room, isolated from her home in North White Plains (a symbolic naming), Avey estimates what was lost when she and Jay moved into sterile middle-class existence. As the winds of the ocean carry the lament of the millions of slaves gone, Avey begins to reconstruct her life.[4]

Avey's presence in the Caribbean triggers personal as well as racial memories, and it is in this environment that Avey begins her middle passage back. Marshall's placing of Avey's awakening in the West Indies has a certain historicity. The different sociohistorical circumstances of the Colonies in the Americas affected dominant views toward the enslaved Africans. For the most part, slavery in the Caribbean allowed for the survival of African cultural traditions in ways that were unthinkable in the "peculiar institution" in the United States. Since the majority of the island plantations were extremely large and most slaves had little contact with the white owners, particularly in the British colonies, African family and societal systems—including language and cultural patterns—remained virtually intact. Slaveowners in the United States, whether for fear of uprisings, domestication, or a misguided sense of Christianity, attempted to destroy all vestiges of African culture. This environment, compounded by a desire for assimilation, helped to alienate African-Americans from their heritage in ways which were not evident in the Caribbean.

In relation to this collective genealogy, Avey's personal historicity stirs up connecting memories: For example, Avey conjures up her great-aunt in a dream after hearing the "patois" which reminds her of the cadences of the voices in Tatem (196). Waiting for a taxi on the wharf, she is called Ida—her physical appearance likened to her unknown Caribbean sister. And her meeting with the ancestor Lebert Joseph gives her an inkling of what has been retained by the Afro-Caribbeans that was lost under the rigid constraints of slavery in the United States. When Lebert Joseph asks Avey, "What's your nation?" she has no idea what he is talking about: "What was the man going on about? What were these names? Did they have something to do with Africa? Senile. The man was senile" (167). At this point, Avey is unable to associate with this heritage, although she has some hint of the names' derivation; in fact, she imposes American dominant discourse on him. In answer to his question, all she can do is call herself a "tourist." Yet she is persuaded by Joseph to take the excursion to the out-island of Carriacou, and through this journey, she reconnects with her collective past.

The boat ride from Grenada to Carriacou is not only a middle passage back but also a *rite de passage* for Avey's spiritual growth. Responding to the rocking of the boat, Avey's semiconscious mind opens to the cultural continuity among those of the diaspora. She compares the wharfside scene to her daughter's slides of a marketplace in Ghana (187); the old ladies on the boat remind her of the "presiding mothers of the Mount Olivet Baptist Church" (194); and the trip itself is reminiscent of a childhood boat ride up the Hudson (188). Finally, her dream revolves around a "call and response" sermon in an African-American church, and her memory of becoming sick in the church sets off an explosion of vomit and diarrhea as Avey undergoes an important purification ritual. This section of the novel is called "Lavé Tête," naming the cleansing ritual and healing practice of "laying on of hands." Under the guidance of the venerable women on the boat, Avey expels all the toxins of her past life, and as her body purges itself, her mind goes through a similar painful healing through the reopening of a collective wound—the Middle Passage: "A multitude it felt lay packed around her in the filth and stench of themselves, just as she was. Their moans . . . their sufferings—the depth of it, the weight of it in the cramped space—made hers of no consequence" (209). Through the stimuli of Lebert Joseph, the maternal sympathies of the old women, and a cleansing bath from Joseph's daughter Rosalie, Avey takes the first step toward wholeness by acknowledging her place in the diaspora.

The final section of the novel is called "The Beg Pardon," and it refers to the ritual of ancestor worship, part of the predominant religious system in West Africa, which has been retained—on both a symbolic and literal level—in much of the New World. In traditional West African cultures, the ancestors "act as official guardians of the social and moral order" (Ray 146). Moreover, as Melville Herskovits points out, "[there is a] widespread belief in the power of the ancestors to affect the lives of their descendants" throughout the diaspora (197). He goes on to say that even though conversion to Christianity has "obliterated overt manifestation of the ancestral cult . . . , the extinction of the cult does not mean that the spirit has disappeared or that its sanctions have not persisted" (199).

Two distinctive American manifestations of ancestor worship are explored in *Praisesong*. In the Caribbean, ancestor worship is direct, whereas the presence of the ancestor in African-American culture exists on a more individualized basis, as a support to a younger relation or friend. Marshall, influenced by both African-American and Caribbean cultures, states in the epigraph to this chapter that she is an "unabashed ancestor worshipper," and she presents a two-fold role for the ancestor in the novel. First, the ancestor functions on a personal level in terms of Avey's growth through the guidance of her dead Aunt Cuney and, to a lesser extent, Lebert Joseph and the physical presence of the elderly matrons on the boat. Second, the ancestor appears as the force of a communal ritual, linking past, present, and future, Africa and the diaspora. When Avey Johnson first hears Lebert Joseph's reasons for the excursion to Carriacou, she does not understand what he is saying, nor can she see any relationship to her own life. He explains that besides the fun and family reunions, the excursion is for "the Old Parents, oui." Then he issues a caveat, mirroring her dream fight with Aunt Cuney: "I tell you, you best remember them! If not they'll get vexed with you and cause you nothing but trouble" (165). Joseph easily fathoms Avey's lack of comprehension concerning her duty to the ancestors because he has children in other lands who have forgotten to give service, and it is clear to us as readers that Avey's denial of her aunt's words and the Ibo ritual service is what causes her discomfort.

After Avey's self-evaluation and cleansing process, she becomes more open to the similarities between the ancestor worship she witnesses in the island of Carriacou and her own family practices back in Tatem. Her new vision is less judgmental than her earlier middle-class myopia, evolved through years of cultural denial. Avey reflects that the ear of corn offered on an altar to the ancestors was "no more strange than the plate of food that used to be placed beside the coffin at funerals in Tatem" (225). Indeed, the tradition of feeding the ancestors is hardly strange in Africa or the diaspora, from Brazil to Harlem, but until this moment, Avey has ignored (been embarrassed by) the cultural practices of her community. With each new awakening, Avey thinks not only of the life and heritage she has left behind, but of the old woman, now dead, who had begged her to remember, and to whom she must now "beg pardon." Like Pilate in *Song of Solomon*, Avey's Great-aunt Cuney is the ancestor and pivotal character of the novel. The elder female figure in the Black family has exerted profound influence in terms of "validation of self and heritage-reminding" on younger relatives and community adolescents (Manns 248). In this novel, though Avey is helped by the old man Lebert Joseph and the old matrons of the island, Great-aunt Cuney has been guide and ancestor throughout Avey's life. Thus, it is pertinent that, throughout Avey's stay in the Caribbean and during the "Nation Dance" at the end of the novel, many of the old and young women as well as Joseph himself function as personae for Great-aunt Cuney. In the course of the novel, Cuney not only appears as Avey's ancestor, she also acts as a presence for the reader, so that we are constantly superimposing Tatem and the African-American experience over the Caribbean scene.

The dream-text at the beginning of the novel prepares us for Avey's conflicting feelings for her Aunt Cuney and the discourse of values that is evoked by it. In the dream discussed earlier in this chapter, Avey angrily resists the pleading Cuney, yet her memories of the old woman expose a child who adored and idealized her great-aunt. And the relationship is no less important to Cuney herself. Naming Avey after her own grandmother Avatara who witnessed the miracle of the Ibos, Cuney believes that Avey is the reincarnation of her gran': "It's my gran' done sent her. She's her little girl" (42). As the discussion in the last chapter indicates, reincarnation is integral to an African world view. Bringing Avey into the world as "Avatara" reflects this heritage as well as the importance of naming:[5] Great-aunt Cuney reminds the child Avey never to forget to say that her name is "Avey, short for Avatara," something Avey, approaching her mid-fifties, has long since forgotten to do. She has not only forgotten to tell people her full name, but she has also disregarded a greater duty to her ancestors, leaving her mission unfulfilled.

Avey's service to her dead ancestor Cuney is intricately linked to the story of the Ibos passed on to Cuney from her gran' Avatara. During her life, Cuney kept the recursive memory of her African heritage alive; most important is the recounting of the legend of the Ibos' walking back to Africa. The tale of the Ibos profoundly affects Cuney's life because she acknowledges her duty to keep the story of Ibo Landing alive and pass it on to the next reincarnated storyteller. A second example further illustrates Cuney's allegiance to her African roots. She starts to cross her feet in church, refusing to deny dance, part of African traditional religion; in doing so, she is kicked out of the "Ring Shout" and eventually leaves the church. Accepting her heritage rather than following the restrictions of the Christian church, Cuney breaks from the Eurocentric imposition of "piety" and chooses to worship at the Landing: "People in Tatem said she had made the Landing her religion after that" (34). The memory of the Ibos and her gran's spiritual journey with them informs this tale with canonical significance as Cuney tells her grandniece Avey about her gran's conversion: "Her body always usta say might be in Tatem but her mind, her mind was long gone with the Ibos" (39). Through Cuney's voice, the legend gains mythic proportions for the young girl. It had taken Avey "years to rid herself of this notion" that she was entrusted with a mission to fulfill (42), yet it is the urgency of this mission which is revisioned in the violent dream battle with Great-aunt Cuney.

Great-aunt Cuney's force resonates in the other characters' relationships with Avey, and much of the imagery surrounding the figures in Carriacou mirrors Cuney's presence. The juxtaposition of the Caribbean "ancestors" who guide Avey through her ordeal at the excursion and the female ancestor who influenced Avey in the past reinforce the generational and cultural continuity of the African diaspora evoked in the novel. Particularly germane to this study is that, with the exception of Lebert Joseph, it is the women who both maintain the traditions and guide Avey to fulfill her mission. The nurturing of Avey by the old women on the boat and later by Joseph's daughter Rosalie reflects the earlier attention of Great-aunt

Cuney. This connection is enhanced by Avey's memories of Cuney's galvanized tub in Tatem as she is being washed by Rosalie (221). Moreover, in a fitful sleep after the ordeal on the boat, Avey perceives Rosalie as the embodiment of Cuney (217). Finally, during the Nation Dance, both a female elder and the young maid watching over Avey remind her of Cuney. Avey watches the young maid enter the floor to join the dance of her tribe: "Her stride as she swiftly crossed to the dancers was that, Avey Johnson thought, of her great-aunt striking out across the fields towards the Landing" (241–42). Still, it is Lebert Joseph, a man—albeit an androgynous, ancient one—who most strongly recalls Great-aunt Cuney's presence. Like Morrison's Pilate, Joseph is a Legba character, a spiritual guide who leads Avey back to her heritage and to the mission she must fulfill for her great-aunt and her foremothers. Moreover, as Velma Pollard notes, Legba is a Dahomean God incarnated in the Caribbean (289), which echoes Avey's earlier desire to be a "Dahomey woman warrior" and save her husband. The opening dedication of the "Lavé Tête" section, "Papa Legba, ouvri barrière pou' mwê," announces the entrance of Joseph. It is he, like Legba, who opens the gates to the world of the ancestors for Avey so that she can articulate and move toward reconciliation of the conflicting aspects of her African-American personality. Joseph resembles Legba in his chameleon-like physical appearance: He is perceived as young, ancient, male, female, short, tall. And most importantly, as in the tradition of possession, he visibly becomes the spirit of Cuney as he guides Avey into acknowledging her duty to future generations. In Avey's first meeting with him, Joseph dances before Avey as her great-aunt had done, performing the Juba—a woman's dance—with an imaginary skirt and feminine movements (178). As he begs her to accompany him on the excursion to Carriacou, his entreaty takes on the urgency of Cuney's grabbing Avey's wrist in the dream: "And although the man had never once touched her, *she felt as if he had reached out and taken her gently but firmly by the wrist*" (183; emphasis added). Finally, at the Nation Dance, Joseph's stance in his "beg pardon" recalls Cuney at Ibo Landing, the first in a line of ancestors to rouse in Avey the memories that have come down in the blood.

The celebration of the Nation Dance is the culmination of Avey's personal awareness, her acknowledgment of her heritage, and the acceptance of her mission. At this point, Marshall links Avey's personal growth with the consciousness of a whole people. Caribbean scholar Carole Boyce Davies comments that the Nation Dance is "a documented ritual enactment of Pan-African unity" and therefore represents the coming together of all those of the African diaspora (41). And the linking of past and present, established in the Nation Dance, also includes the unborn, those witnesses for the future, on whom the burden of the stories and the traditions rests.

The festival itself, honoring the dead ancestors and the African nations the slaves came from, is a New World ritual based on African traditions and festivals that exist now only in memory. And the ceremony has resonances of the New Life festival in *Foriwa*, in which the traditions and practices of the ancestors give sustenance and social responsibility to the descendants. The "Big Drum," composed of the singing of songs and the dancing (not allowed in Cuney's church), underscores this Pan-African connection. Paul Carter Harrison emphasizes these aspects of transformed African culture in New World Black life: "Song, Dance and Drum are as important to the modes of contemporary Black experience as they always have been in traditional African life. While the New World may have colored these expressive indices, the resonances of Africa remain apparent" (22). As illustrated by the Nation Dance and the novel as a whole, ties to African heritage are more clearly articulated by those descendants in the Caribbean. Still, these cultural traditions, colored by the African-American experience, become more readily apparent through Avey's (re)memory of her past.

In the Nation Dance, the oldest member of a tribe or nation starts the dance in honor of the dead and the memory of that ancestry. After the dancing is the "Beg Pardon" in which the living ask for atonement from the ancestors and beg forgiveness for those who no longer remember—"the sons and daughters, grands and great-grands in Trinidad, Toronto, New York, London" (236). Since these "far-flung kin" are the ones most likely to forget, the old ones pray twice as hard to protect them. But the elders' greatest fear is that these sons and daughters will not be able to pass on the traditions of the tribe to future generations and the continuum will be broken. Avey is conscious of the ancientness of the bodies who conduct the "Beg Pardon" as she witnesses the "Big Drum." This realization creates an awareness of the urgency of their commitment and the growing of her own:

It was the essence of something rather than the thing itself that she was witnessing. All that was left were a few names of what they called nations which they could no longer even pronounce properly, the fragments of a dozen or so songs, the shadowing forms of long-ago dances.... *And they clung to them with a tenacity she suddenly loved in them and longed for in herself.* (240; emphasis added)

At this point, Avey's reassessment of her life comes to fruition; through her (re)memory of the past, she is prepared for her and her children's future. Her growing awareness of the strength which resides in this cognizance is emphasized in her realization that it is not necessary to know specifically one's tribe or one's long-ago ancestors. What is important—evoked also in *Song of Solomon*—is to be part of this collective memory and have the tenacity, in spite of the opposition, to pass on the stories and traditions to future gene- rations. Avey's comprehension of this world view is partially derived from her feeling of "dwelling in any number of places at once" during the celebration (232). As she once felt joined to the people on the boat ride up the Hudson, she glories in the invisible threads connecting her to the people around her, bridging the gap between her and all those who share her cultural heritage: ancestor, contem- porary, and descendant. Two incidents make it clear to us that Avey has done more than just passively accept the African heritage she has long denied--her participation in the Nation Dance and her accept- ance of her ancestral name. As she wonders whether she should join the dancers, she feels a final burst of resistance from that bourgeois, restrictive, alienated woman within her. She hears the voice of her husband, Jay, over the music and dancing: "*If it was left to me, I'd close down every dance hall in Harlem and burn every drum!*" (247). But Avey is no longer dominated by that voice nor by the hege- monic culture that fashioned it: She takes a step forward into the ring and dances with the others, the dance that her great-aunt was condemned to dance alone. For the first time since childhood, Avey feels the diasporal threads "streaming out of everyone there to enter her, making her part of what seemed a far-reaching, wide-ranging confraternity" (249).

This powerful climax is underscored by Avey's readoption of her ancestral name, Avatara: "And as a mystified Avey Johnson gave her name, she suddenly remembered her Great-aunt Cuney's admonishment long ago" (251). As the reincarnation of her great-aunt's gran', Avey accepts her mission to pass on the story of the Ibos to her own and other children of the community. Finally, as Avey listens to the song, dance, and drum of the festival, she comes to realize the full extent of her collective memory and the ability of those of the diaspora to transform the suffering into beauty through song—as Morrison writes, "the plea into a note": "The note was a lamentation that could hardly have come from the rum keg of a drum. Its source had to be the heart, the bruised, still-bleeding innermost chamber of the collective heart" (244–45). For Marshall and for her character Avey Johnson, the ability to transform tragedy into beauty on a communal level is what must be transmitted, even in more affluent times. And for Avey, her journey has bent her to the traditions of her foremothers and has led her from division toward wholeness.[6]

Like characters in Marshall's other novels, Avey grows as a woman and a member of a "tribe" by the end of the book. She returns home not only with a greater awareness of her own life but also with a cognizance of how that life is part of the community's life. *Praisesong* is Marshall's most realized exploration of personal growth within the sociohistorical context of the African diaspora. The protagonist Avey Johnson accepts her mission to pass on the story of her African forebears to the young, placing her squarely within the tradition of African women storytellers and the women of her own extended family. As the direct beneficiary of the precious tale of transcendence and survival, Avey has a duty to prepare future generations to combat the oppression and alienation in their lives and to be actively involved in the African-American community. Avey begins her strategy as she flies back to the United States: First, she will tell her own children the story which has been hidden through years of denial; second, she will enlist her daughter Marion to help share the knowledge with the larger community. Avey chooses to pass on her mission to Marion—who understood the importance of their African heritage despite her parents' rejection—just as Great-aunt Cuney chose Avey: "Of her three children, Marion alone would understand about the excursion and help her spread the word" (255). Just as the African woman is responsible for the education of all the children of her community, Avey is determined to reach more children than just her own. She expands her territory from suburban White Plains to the "canyon streets and office buildings" of Manhattan, where she will halt the "young, bright, fiercely articulate token few for whom her generation had worked the two and three jobs . . . and quote the line from her namesake" (255). Avey takes her mission beyond the Sea Island community in which her great-aunt lived to a larger community in the urban North, just as Marshall herself has brought the wisdom of the poets in the kitchen to a broader audience, sending the message outward in concentric circles. The process that Avey Johnson has gone through is one with which all members of oppressed groups must wrestle if they are ever to achieve an integrated sense of self. Marshall clearly states that objective in "Shaping the World of My Art":

> An oppressed people cannot overcome their oppressors and take control of their lives until they have a clear and truthful picture of all that has gone before, until they begin to use their history creatively. This knowledge of one's culture, one's history, serves as an ideological underpinning for the political, social and economic battles they must wage. It is the base upon which they must build. (107)

In *Praisesong*, Marshall explores the transition of one woman from a discarder of heritage to a (re)builder of cultural history. By her spiritual middle passage back through the Caribbean, Avey Johnson not only moves toward the integration of her divided self, she also makes a commitment to pass on the stories and traditions to those who do not, or refuse to, remember. Marshall presents a discourse to resolve the warring conflicts of the African and American self, while articulating the dialectics of that double-self, through the acceptance of the wisdom of the ancestors. And as all the writers examined in this study, Marshall praises the women who have passed on this heritage to subsequent generations.

# Conclusion

*Bila asili utumwa*
(One who knows not one's origin is
doomed to servitude)

Swahili proverb

■ The historicity of the late twentieth century has inscribed in many a desire to examine their roots, to (re)define origin.
Encoded in this desire is an inequality; for some (the elite of the
dominant culture), their past is documented, crested, historicized.
For those of oppressed cultures, diasporal ones, their historicity is
encoded in cultural imperatives, remembered in collective rather
than individual terms. Sometimes it is a recursive fragment, as Henry
Louis Gates, Jr. notes, which needs reassemblage—for connection
to the source can bring power (the slaveowners knew this; that is
why they tried to efface every aspect of African culture in the slave
communities). As the Swahili proverb tells us, to be denied heritage
is to be denied freedom. Paul Carter Harrison comments on the
essentiality of African heritage as a trope for Black Aesthetic art:

> It is the source that gives expression to our walk/dance, talk/song,
> provides rhythm/silence at the Sunday chicken dinner table, urban/
> rural: all of it must be attended in a manner which creates the
> strongest reality of our power to summon the dynamics of Black life
> into harmonious relationships with the mode. (29)

Committed Black writers and critics today have expanded on the
concept of a Black aesthetic to create an African aesthetic in exploring the Black American oral/literary tradition in the United States.[1]
For many Black women writers, this attention to one's African cul-

tural heritage has also included a reaching out to one's African and Caribbean sisters as part of a diaspora literature.

In Africa and its diaspora, reconstructing history has been involved with an uncovering of heritage, a laying bare of the original material of culture as well as a layering of emergent cultural traditions which oppose Eurocentric hegemony. The writers in this study have written emergent literature based on the residual cultural practices of an African past. As Abena P. B. Busia lucidly states, this (re)memory is not retrogressive: "The past is not reclaimed for its own sake but because without a recognition of it, there can be no understanding of the present and no future" (27). For these authors, there is a determination to find a "usable past," which is neither glorified nor defiled, and to create an atmosphere of liberation, negating inscribed racism and sexism. The works examined in this study, by women on both sides of the Atlantic, not only attest to the continuation of African cultural heritage in the Americas as well as in Africa but also clarify how these values have been passed on by women through generations and the Middle Passage. Their critical and creative stance has been directed toward the manner in which those cultural traditions have been imparted. They underscore the primary role of their foremothers—as well as their own role to our community of readers—in keeping those traditions alive.

In *Women's Ways of Knowing*, Mary Field Belenky et al. define alternative ways of *knowing* that women, as a group, have and which may differ from the world as defined by men. Bernice Johnson Reagon points out that women, in this case women of the African diaspora, may have other ways of *telling* as well. These mothering ways of telling are intricately related to ways of knowing and passing on that knowledge to future generations. In this way, the search for selfhood of person and nation is "integrally tied to the creation of stories" (Busia 3). Through the telling of the stories—and this is what writers do—the authors discussed in this book extend the cultural practices of the communities to the words on a page. In their oraliterature, they move from their communities to the community of readers. And the traditions they (re)create and the methods they use are not static but are constantly renewed by the flow of voices that remember other stories and create them anew.

This study contributes to the growing dialogue between women writers and critics of the African diaspora by examining six writers in terms of not only the cultural connections that exist but also the ways those cultural imperatives have been mothered into being. The African women writers' aims are directed toward building societies which function by constantly renewed cultural traditions; furthermore, they emphasize the reforming of these traditions to (re)-acknowledge women's place as full citizens within the context of these new societies. This goal is best exemplified by the reviving of the New Life festival in *Foriwa*. The African-American women writers' work aims toward a rearticulation of the double-self, not as opposing forces but as dialectical existence, especially in terms of the recognition of the African folk heritage and the women who have passed on the stories of their suffering and strength to their children. Moreover, these writers also affirm the place of Black women, not merely as brutalized victims, but as creative artists who have constantly fought not only the racism of the dominant culture but also the sexism of their own men. Finally, Marshall's rendition of Aunt Cuney, who relates the story of the Ibos to her grand-niece Avey, is a paradigm for the cultural ties which have spanned time and the Atlantic.

In their oraliterature, these six women have told the story of their heritage to the children, the community, the audience, and the reader, just as their women characters pass on the cultural practices and traditions within the world of each book. For even in their differences in approach as well as in culture, country, and continent, these writers' roles as African women storytellers and their diasporal commitment to tell the tale have remained constant. To return to the Swahili proverb, attention to one's stories, traditions, and heritage may have helped women of Africa and the diaspora to survive the horrors of servitude and slavery and enabled them to keep the notion of their origins alive. With the emergence of the contemporary Black woman writer on both sides of the Atlantic, we are presented with a (re)vision of the bonds existing between Africans and African-Americans as well as the significant voice of women in maintaining and strengthening those cultural ties. In their own voice, these women writers have confronted the sources of oppression, and they have identified generational and cultural continuity—passed on by women—as the construct which has held their communities together. Trinh T. Minh-ha tells us that the "world's earliest archives or libraries were the memories of women" (121). Through these writers' recursive journey into their foremothers' orature, they have documented this mothering process of cultural transmission and have celebrated the women in their communities and the diaspora, past and present, who have kept these traditions alive.

# NOTES

## Introduction

1. I am grateful to Beverly Stoeltje, University of Texas, for supplying me with the term "generational continuity."

2. My use of the terms "Eurocentric" and "Afrocentric" comes from the critical terminology used by Chinweizu, Jemie, and Maduibuike, *Towards the Decolonization of African Literature* (Washington, DC: Howard UP, 1983) 3.

3. I prefer Robinson's term "excluded" for the literatures of oppressed groups because the other terms—"nontraditional," "marginal," "minority"—do not clearly state the process in which these writers have been ignored.

4. Most of the book-length studies of Black Feminist criticism by African-Americans are cited in the text. One work which exemplifies the broad-based and sometimes oppositional critical approaches to Black women's literature is *Changing Our Own Words*, ed. Cheryl Wall. There is also forefront critical work being done by African and Caribbean women such as writers Ama Ata Aidoo and Micere Mugo (Kenya) and critics Omolara Ogundipe-Leslie (Nigeria), Juliet Okonkwo (Nigeria), and Maryse Condé (Guadaloupe).

5. The term "cultural preparedness" comes from Robert Thompson's *The Flash of the Spirit* (New York: Random House, 1984), which examines artistic traditions which, without being "taught," are encoded in the culture. See also Gerhard Kubik, *Angolan Traits in Black Music, Games, and Dances of Brazil* (Lisbon: Centro de Studios des Antropologia Cultura, 1979).

6. Recent studies have indicated the importance of the Bantu-speaking people of Central Africa as well as the Africans along the west coast in terms of cultural retentions. See, for example, studies by Molefi Ketu Asante and Robert Farris Thompson and the collection *Africanisms in American Culture*, ed. Joseph E. Holloway (Bloomington: Indiana University Press, 1990).

7. My term "oraliterature" is similar to Gates's concept of the "speakerly text" in his study *The Signifying Monkey*. While Gates's focus is on the "representation of the speaking black voice in writing," mine is

more on the inscription of the orature in the written text.

8. For a fuller discussion of the problems associated with this work, see—among others—my review of *Female Novelists of Modern Africa* in *Research in African Literatures* 16.4 (1985): 604–607.

9. For example, A. C. Jordan, in *Tales from Southern Africa*, comments that it was usually the men who told animal tales, whereas "women, especially the older women, are said to have excelled in the interpretation of tales dealing with human subjects" (xix).

10. Chinua Achebe refers to this aspect of Igbo cosmology in *Morning Yet on Creation Day* (161). This traditional African world view is later explored in post–World War II Marxist philosophy. For example, Theodor Adorno states in *Negative Dialectics*, "What is, is more than it is" (161).

11. See, for example, Ivan Van Sertima, *They Came Before Columbus* (New York: Random House, 1976), Bernard Makhosezwe Magubane, *The Ties that Bind* (Trenton, NJ: Africa World Press, 1987) and Holloway, *Africanisms in American Culture*, cited above. Literary criticism like *The Signifying Monkey* and other works cited in the text as well as conferences like "The Black Woman Writer and the Diaspora," held at Michigan State U in 1986, also reflect this trend.

12. One of the layers of my own discussion here has been developed by my reading of the study *Women's Ways of Knowing* by psychologists Belenky, Clinchy, Goldberger, and Tarule. Although they focus on American women within a Western philosophical context, their development of the ways women know can easily be applied to this study. The authors state that the work describes "the ways of knowing that women have cultivated and learned to value, ways we have come to believe are powerful but have been neglected and denigrated by the dominant intellectual ethos of our time" (iv). What is most applicable to this study is the concept of "constructed knowledge" which integrates subjective/objective understanding of the world around them—and through the constructing of knowledge once denied, the women help to make the world of their communities "more livable" (152).

13. Frazier's view was refuted by anthropologist Melville Herskovits in *The Myth of the Negro Past* in 1941. Ladner and other modern sociologists who see Black family organization as a direct result of their African descent are cited in the text. In a recent interview with Will Nixon, novelist David Bradley responded negatively to Gates and others' claim of an African oral tradition informing Black literature.

14. Both Lloyd Brown in "The African Heritage and the Harlem Renaissance" and Ezekiel Mphahlele in *The African Image* comment on the "sentimental idealism" of Renaissance writers Hughes, Cullen, and McKay. Unfortunately, neither scholar mentions Hurston's work as a radically different approach to understanding one's African heritage.

15. For the most blatant example of the "pathology" brand of sociology, see Daniel Moynihan's *The Negro Family: A Case for National Action.*

16. Ironically, this strength of the Black woman has been seen by quite

a few Black writers (mostly male) as suffocating dominance. See, for example, Daryl Dance, "Black Eve or Madonna: A Study of the Antithetical Views of the Mother in Black American Literature."

## 1. Flora Nwapa, *Efuru*

1. Flora Nwapa, personal interview, Enugu, Nigeria, 3 June 1984. I am extremely grateful to Flora Nwapa for our many conversations and my trip to Oguta during my stay in Nigeria.

2. For a discussion of Palmer's critical approach, see Chinweizu 98; 136–45.

3. Because of the rules of exogamy, women could not marry men from their own clan or village, so they had to marry outside. The marriage in turn would build alliances between the two communities.

4. For a male perspective of the opposition of children and wealth with regard to the water deity, see Chinua Achebe's short story "Uncle Ben's Choice," in *Girls at War* (London: Heinemann, 1972).

## 2. Efua Sutherland, *Foriwa*

1. See E. Ofori Okyea, "The Atwia-Ekumfi Kodzidan—An Experimental African Theatre," *Okyeame* 4.1 (1970): 82–85.

2. An excellent treatment of this topic is Ada Mere's unpublished paper "The Unique Role of Women in Nation Building." See also, "Women: The Neglected Human Resource for African Development," *Journal of African Studies* 1.2 (1972): 359–70.

3. In "The Black Woman in History" (*Black World* 24.4 [1975]: 12–26), John Henrik Clarke states that from the time of the traders, the colonialists "began a war on African customs, religion and cultures. In most cases, the first custom they attacked was the matriarchy. . . ." See also Cheikh Anta Diop, *The Cultural Unity of Black Africa* (Chicago: Third World Press, 1959) and Kamene Okonjo, "Sex Roles in Nigerian Politics" in Oppong 212–21.

4. For a British woman's reflections on the demise of the women's courts and women's political power under British occupation, see Sylvia Leith-Ross, *African Women* (London: Routledge, 1939).

5. I am freely paraphrasing from a passage in Jane Marcus's "Still Practice A/Wrested Alphabet: Towards a Feminist Aesthetic," quoted in the introduction.

## 3. Ama Ata Aidoo, *The Dilemma of a Ghost*

1. Dr. Kwegyir Aggrey made this statement concerning women's important role in the development of Ghana. Ama Ata Aidoo cites him in the

notes to her speech "Unwelcome Pals and Decorative Slaves," *Medium and Message* 35.

2. Revealingly, Ghanaian critic Abena Busia remarks that Cape Coast and Elmina were both active slave ports during the trade.

3. See Aidoo's interview with Theo Vincent as well as her commentary at the first meeting of the African Literature Association Conference at Northwestern University. The issue of whether to write in an African or colonial language is discussed at length in the publication of this conference.

4. See, for example, John Nagenda, "Generations in Conflict," *Protest and Conflict in African Literature*, ed. Munro and Pieterse (New York: Africana Publishing Corp., 1969), especially p. 107.

5. There has been quite a bit of negative criticism on Eulalie as a realistic character, particularly Aidoo's inability to capture Eulalie's accent realistically. Although I agree that Eulalie's Black English is stilted, I am not sure that this discredits her as a realistic character, as critics such as Maryse Condé and Brenda Berrian suggest.

6. W. E. B. Dubois examines this conflict in "On Spiritual Striving," in *The Souls of Black Folk* (New York: New American Library, 1953).

### 4. Alice Walker, *The Color Purple*

1. In the opening of *In Search of Our Mothers' Gardens*, Walker explains that "womanist" comes from the Black folk term "womanish" and refers to a Black feminist or feminist of color.

2. Deborah E. McDowell makes an interesting case for Francis Harper's influence on Walker as well, particularly in the "Nettie" sections of the novel, in "'The Changing Same': Generational Connections and Black Women Novelists," *New Literary History* 18.2 (1987): 281–302.

3. At the end of *The Color Purple,* Walker refers to herself as medium and thanks everyone in the book for coming (253).

4. Although this study does not include Walker's most recent novel, *The Temple of My Familiar*, certainly there is more than enough material for a sustained analysis of the role of Africa and African heritage in this work (including the examination of the two sisters, African and African-American, Nzingha and Fanny Nzingha).

5. In "Support Systems of Significant Others in Black Families," Wilhelmina Manns defines this term as an elder or peer who exists as a strong social support for another individual. In this essay, she examines the predominance of this type of role model in African-American communities.

6. See, for example, Mel Watkins's review and Trudier Harris's generally harsh criticism of the novel. For a response on the "formalness" of the prose in these sections, see McDowell above. Two recent studies by Molly Hite and Elliott Butler-Evans (cited in this chapter) have presented more favorable readings of these sections.

7. In some West African cultures, looking down at the ground is a sign

of respect. I recall a discussion I had in Nigeria with Igbo sociologist Kamene Okonjo, who felt that Western feminists were constantly misreading the relationship between African men and women. She mentioned that the fact that men and women do not usually go out together was cited by some Western feminists as an example of women's secondary position because the men would not *take* their wives along. Rather, she explained, the women have their own activities and often *prefer* the company of other women for these events.

8. This notion of the utopian vision as counterhegemonic comes from a workshop on Frantz Fanon, conducted by Abdul JanMohammed, African Literature Association Conference, Michigan State U, 17 April 1986.

## 5. Toni Morrison, *Song of Solomon*

1. See, for example, Jean Strouse, "Toni Morrison's Black Magic," *Newsweek*, 30 March 1981: 52. Fortunately, the privileging of Western culture and written text over African cultural traditions and orature has changed since Black/Feminist critics cited in this study have been exploring these works. One related example is Vashti Crutcher Lewis's "African Traditions in Toni Morrison's *Sula*."

2. Caribbean writer and scholar Wilson Harris referred to this phenomenon in a seminar at the University of Texas, Spring 1983. There are many references to this legend in the WPA oral history, *Drums and Shadows*, examined more fully in the next chapter. Other sources include Julius Lester, "People Who Could Fly" 147–52, J. Mason Brewer, "Flying People" 309, and Virginia Hamilton's *People Who Could Fly*. For further analysis of this legend with regard to Black American writers, see my "If You Surrender to the Air: Legends of Flight and Resistance in African-American Writers," in *MELUS* 16.1 (1989–90): 21–32.

3. This is a paraphrase of a statement by Walter Ong, discussed in the introduction.

4. Kathleen O'Shaughnessy, in "'Life Life Life Life': The Community as Chorus in *Song of Solomon*," examines Morrison's use of chorus within the context of the book but does not expand this notion to include the readers.

5. John Edgar Wideman refers to this practice in his novel *Damballah*: "It was customary for slaves to disregard the cumbersome, ironic names bestowed by whites, and rechristen one another in a secret, second language, a language whose forms and words gave substance to the captives' need to see themselves as human beings" (195).

6. Discussions with Donatus Nwoga, February–March 1983. At the time, Nwoga was working on an article seriously appraising the concept of reincarnation within the context of modern African society. One example of reincarnation in contemporary African literature is Buchi Emecheta's *The Joys of Motherhood* (New York: George Braziller, 1979), in which the main protagonist, Nnu Ego, is the reincarnation of a slave girl forced by

Nnu Ego's family to die.

## 6. Paule Marshall, *Praisesong for the Widow*

1. The term "Middle Passage back" comes from Mary Helen Washington, "Afterword," *Brown Girl, Brownstones* (1959; Old Westbury, NY: Feminist Press, 1981) 311–24, esp. p. 324.

2. I heard Marshall read the Ibo section of *Praisesong* at the NWSA convention, Ohio U, 26 June 1982, and I was reminded of the master storytellers whose recitations are heard throughout the villages of West Africa. I am also grateful to Marshall for conversations we had during her trip to Greenville, NC, March 1988.

3. I have used two spellings of "Igbo" in this chapter. I used the above phonetic spelling (generally acknowledged as preferable) in discussion of the group, but I have used "Ibo" in reference to the work and the transformative changes that are present in the Americas.

4. This image of the ocean as a remembrance of the trauma of slavery is derived from Marshall's second novel, *The Chosen Place, the Timeless People* 106.

5. According to Keith A. Sandiford, the name Avatara may come from the root word "avatar," meaning the "incarnation of a deity." This reinforces the sense of reincarnation in the novel and also evokes "Avatara's role as a representative rather than an individual life" (391). Thus, the notion of collective memory is strengthened. Furthermore, editor and friend Kathy Whaley pointed out that the verb "avatarati" (s/he descends) includes the root word "tarati"—s/he crosses over. So many connections!

6. This is a paraphrase from Eugenia Collier, "The Closing of the Circle: Movement from Division to Wholeness in Paule Marshall's Fiction." As I have noted, whether there can be a complete sense of wholeness in the "double-self" is still an open question. The novel does not end on a static note but rather it poses a dialectic, with Avey at the beginning/end of a search.

## Conclusion

1. I have taken the term "African Aesthetics" as a development of Black Aesthetics from Mildred Hill-Lubin, "The Influence of African Aesthetics on the Work of Paule Marshall," African Literature Association Conference, Michigan State U, 18 April 1986.

# WORKS CITED AND
# SELECT BIBLIOGRAPHY

Abrahams, Roger. *African Folktales.* New York: Pantheon Books, 1983.
Abu, Katherine. "The Separateness of Spouses: Conjugal Resources in an Ashanti Town." *Female and Male in West Africa.* Ed. Christine Oppong. London: George Allen, 1983. 156–68.
Achebe, Chinua. *Girls at War.* London: Heinemann, 1972.
———. *Morning Yet on Creation Day.* London: Heinemann, 1975.
———. Personal interview. 7 March 1984.
Adedeji, Joel. "Theatre and Ideology in Africa." *Joliso* 2.1 (1974): 72–82.
Adelugba, Dapo. "Language and Drama: Ama Ata Aidoo." *African Literature Today* 8 (1976): 72–84.
Adorno, Theodor. *Negative Dialectics.* London: Routledge, 1973.
Aidoo, Agnes Akosua. "Asante Queen Mothers in Government and Politics in the Nineteenth Century." Steady 65–78.
Aidoo, Ama Ata. *Anowa.* London: Longman, 1970.
———. *The Dilemma of a Ghost.* London: Longman, 1965.
———. Interview. With Maxine Lautré. Duerden 19–27.
———. *No Sweetness Here.* London: Longman, 1970.
———. *Our Sister Killjoy.* Lagos: Nok Publishers, 1979.
———. "Roundtable Discussion." First African Literature Association Conference, Northwestern University. *Issue* 6.1 (1976): 124–27.
———. "Unwelcome Pals and Decorative Slaves." *Medium and Message.* Proc. of the International Conference on African Literature and the English Language, U of Calabar, Nigeria, 1980. 17–37.
Anyidoho, Kofi. Personal interview. 14 Nov. 1982.
Anzaldua, Gloria, and Cherrie Moraga, eds. *This Bridge Called My Back: Radical Writings of Women of Color.* Watertown, MA: Persephone Press, 1981.
Arhin, Kwame. "The Political and Military Role of Akan Women." Oppong 92–98.
Asagba, Austin Ovigueraye. "Roots of African Drama: Critical Approaches and Elements of Continuity." *Kunapipi* 8.3 (1986): 84–99.
Avery, Greta. "African Oral Traditions." *Africana Research Bulletin* 1.1 (1970): 17–36.
Awoonor, Kofi. *The Breast of the Earth.* New York: Doubleday, 1975.
Babb, Valerie, "*The Color Purple*: Writing to Undo What Writing Has Done." *Phylon* 47.2 (1986): 107–16.

Bakhtin, M. M. *The Dialogic Imagination*. Trans. and ed. Michael Holquist. Austin: U of Texas P, 1981.

Bambara, Toni Cade. *The Salt Eaters*. New York: Random House, 1980.

Banham, M. J., and Clive Wake. *African Theatre Today*. London: Pitman Press, 1976.

Bascom, William. *African Dilemma Tales*. The Hague: Mouton, 1975.

Belenky, Mary Field, Blythe McVicker Clinchy, Nancy Rule Goldberger, and Jill Mattuck Tarule. *Women's Ways of Knowing*. New York: Basic Books, 1986.

Berrian, Brenda. "The Afro-American—West African Marriage Question: Its Literary and Historical Contexts." *African Literature Today* 15 (1987): 152–59.

———. *Bibliography of African Women Writers and Journalists*. Washington, DC: Three Continents Press, 1985.

Bethel, Lorraine. "This Infinity of Conscious Pain." Hull 176–88.

Bradley, David. Interview. With Will Nixon. *Poets & Writers* 18.4 (1990): 29–34.

Brewer, J. Mason. *American Negro Folklore*. New York: Quadrangle Press, 1968.

Brown, Lloyd. "The African Heritage and the Harlem Renaissance." *African Literature Today* 9 (1978): 1–10.

———. *Women Writers of Black Africa*. Westport, CT: Greenwood Press, 1981.

Bruner, Charlotte. "Been-To or Has-Been: A Dilemma for Today's African Woman." *Ba Shiru* 8.2 (1977): 21–30.

Busia, Abena P. B. "Words Whispered over Voids: A Context for Black Women's Rebellious Voices in the Novel of the African Diaspora." *Black Feminist Criticism and Critical Theory*. Ed. Houston A. Baker and Joe Weixlmann. *Studies in Black American Literature*. Vol. 3. Greenville, FL: Penkeville Publishing, 1987. 1–41.

Butler-Evans, Elliott. "Beyond Essentialism: Rethinking Afro-American Cultural Theory." *Inscriptions* 5 (1989): 121–34.

———. *Race, Gender, and Desire: Narrative Strategies in the Fiction of Toni Cade Bambara, Toni Morrison, and Alice Walker*. Philadelphia: Temple UP, 1989.

Chapman, Karen. "Introduction to Ama Ata Aidoo's *Dilemma of a Ghost*." *Sturdy Black Bridges*. Ed. Roseann P. Bell, Bettye J. Parker, and Beverly Guy-Sheftall. New York: Doubleday, 1979. 25–38.

Cheung, King-Kok. "'Don't Tell': Imposed Silences in *The Color Purple* and *The Woman Warrior*. *PMLA* 103.2 (1988): 162–74.

Chinweizu, Onwuchekwa Jemie, and Ihechukwu Maduibuike. *Towards the Decolonization of African Literature*. Washington, DC: Howard UP, 1983.

Christian, Barbara. "Alice Walker: The Black Woman Artist as Wayward." Evans 457–77.

———. *Black Feminist Criticism*. New York: Pergamon Press, 1985.

Clark, J. P. *Three Plays*. Oxford: Oxford UP, 1964.

Clarke, John Henrik. "The Black Woman in History." *Black World* 24.4 (1975): 12–26.

Collier, Eugenia. "The Closing of the Circle: Movement from Division to

Wholeness in Paule Marshall's Fiction." Evans 295–315.

Condé, Maryse. "Three Female Writers in Modern Africa." *Presence Africaine* 82 (1972): 136–39.

Crane, Louise. *Ms. Africa*. New York: Lippincott, 1973.

Dance, Daryl. "Black Eve or Madonna: A Study of the Antithetical Views of the Mother in Black American Literature." *Perspectives on Afro-American Women*. Ed. Willa D. Johnson and Thomas L. Green. Washington, DC: ECCA Publications, 1975. 103–11.

Davies, Carole Boyce. "Motherhood in the Works of Male and Female Igbo Writers." Davies and Graves, 241–56.

———. "Mothering and Healing in Recent Black Women's Fiction." *Sage* 2.1 (1985): 41–43.

Davies, Carole Boyce, and Anne Adams Graves, eds. *Ngambika: Studies of Women in African Literature*. Trenton, NJ: Africa World Press, 1986.

Diop, Cheikh Anta. *The Cultural Unity of Black Africa*. Chicago: Third World Press, 1959.

*Drums and Shadows: Survival Studies among the Georgia Coastal Negroes*. Savannah Unit, Georgia Writer's Project. Athens: U of Georgia, 1940.

DuBois, W. E. B. *The Souls of Black Folk*. New York: New American Library, 1953.

Duerden, Dennis, and Cosmos Pieterse, eds. *African Writers Talking*. New York: Africana Publishing, 1972.

Eko, Ebele. "Beyond the Myth of Confrontation: A Comparative Study of African and African-American Female Protagonists." *Ariel* 17.4 (1986): 139–52.

Emecheta, Buchi. *The Joys of Motherhood*. New York: George Braziller, 1979.

———. *Our Own Freedom*. London: Sheba Feminist Publishers, 1981.

Emenyonu, Ernest. "Who Does Flora Nwapa Write For?" *African Literature Today* 7 (1975): 28–33.

Evans, Mari, ed. *Black Women Writers (1950–1980): A Critical Evaluation*. New York: Anchor Books, 1984.

Fanon, Frantz. *The Wretched of the Earth*. Trans. Constance Farrington. New York: Grove Press, 1968.

Farrer, Claire, ed. *Women and Folklore*. Austin: U of Texas P, 1975.

Finnegan, Ruth. *Oral Literature in Africa*. Oxford: Oxford UP, 1970.

Frazier, E. Franklin. *The Negro Family in the United States*. Chicago: U of Chicago P, 1939.

Gates, Henry Louis, Jr. *The Signifying Monkey*. New York: Oxford UP, 1988.

Graham-White, Anthony. *The Drama of Black Africa*. New York: Samuel French, 1974.

Green, M. M. *Igbo Village Affairs*. London: Frank Cass, 1947.

Haley, Alex. Personal interview. 19 Feb. 1986.

———. *Roots*. New York: Doubleday, 1986.

———. "Search for an Ancestor." *American Vistas*. Ed. Leonard Dinnerstein and Kenneth Jackson. New York: Oxford UP, 1975. 221–31.

Hamilton, Virginia. *People Who Could Fly*. New York: Knopf, 1985.

Harris, Trudier. "On *The Color Purple*, Stereotypes and Silence." *Black American Literature Forum* 18.4 (1984): 155–61.

Harris, Wilson. *Explorations.* Ed. Hena Maes-Jelinek. Aarhus, Denmark: Dangaroo Press, 1981.

Harrison, Paul Carter, ed. *Kuntu Drama.* New York: Grove Press, 1974.

Herskovits, Melville. *The Myth of the Negro Past.* Boston: Beacon Press, 1941.

Hill-Lubin, Mildred. "The Grandmother in African and African-American Literature." Davies and Graves 257–70.

———. "The Influence of African Aesthetics on the Works of Paule Marshall." African Literature Association Conference, Michigan State U. 18 April 1986.

Hite, Molly. "Romance, Marginality, Matrilineage: Alice Walker's *The Color Purple* and Zora Neale Hurston's *Their Eyes Were Watching God.*" *Novel: A Forum on Fiction* 22.3 (1989): 257–73.

Holloway, Joseph E. *Africanisms in American Culture.* Bloomington: Indiana University Press, 1990.

Hull, Gloria T., Patricia Bell Scott, and Barbara Smith, eds. *All the Women Are White, All the Blacks Are Men, BUT SOME OF US ARE BRAVE.* Old Westbury, NY: Feminist Press, 1982.

Hurston, Zora Neale. *Their Eyes Were Watching God.* Urbana: U of Illinois P, 1937.

Jameson, Frederic. *Marxism and Form.* Princeton: Princeton UP, 1971.

Jordan, A. C. *Tales from Southern Africa.* Berkeley: U of California P, 1973.

July, Robert W. *An African Voice: The Role of the Humanities in African Independence.* Durham: Duke UP, 1987.

Kilson, Marion. *Royal Antelope and Spider.* London: Cambridge UP, 1976.

———. "Women and African Literature." *Journal of African Studies* 4.2 (1977): 161–66.

Kubik, Gerhard. *Angolan Traits in Black Music, Games, and Dances of Brazil.* Lisbon: Centro de Studios des Antropologia Cultura, 1979.

Ladner, Joyce. "Racism and Tradition: Black Womanhood in Historical Perspective." Steady 269–88.

———. *Tomorrow's Tomorrow.* New York: Doubleday, 1972.

Lautré, Maxine. "Interview with Ama Ata Aidoo." Duerden 19–27.

LeClair, Thomas. "The Language Must Not Sweat." *The New Republic* 21 March 1981: 25–32.

Lee, Dorothy, H. "The Quest for Self: Triumph and Failure in the Works of Toni Morrison." Evans 346–60.

Leith-Ross, Sylvia. *African Women.* London: Routledge, 1939.

Lester, Julius. *Black Folktales.* New York: Grove Press, 1969.

Lewis, Vashti Crutcher. "African Traditions in Toni Morrison's *Sula.*" *Wild Women in the Whirlwind: Afra-American Culture and the Contemporary Literary Renaissance.* Ed. Joanne M. Braxton and Andrée Nicola McLaughlin. New Brunswick: Rutgers UP, 1990.

Lindfors, Bernth. "Achebe's Followers." *Revue de Littérature Comparée* 48 (1974): 569–78.

———. *Black African Literature in English*. Detroit: Gale Research, 1979.

———. "The Image of the Afro-American in African Literature." *Association for Commonwealth Literature and Language Studies Bulletin* 4.3 (1975): 19–26.

Mack, Beverly. "Songs from Silence: Hausa Women's Poetry." Davies and Graves 181–90.

Magubane, Bernard Makhosezwe. *The Ties that Bind: African-American Consciousness of Africa*. Trenton, NJ: Africa World Press, 1987.

Manns, Wilhelmina. "Support Systems of Significant Others in Black Families." McAdoo 237–49.

Marcus, Jane. "Still Practice A/Wrested Alphabet: Towards a Feminist Aesthetic." *Tulsa Studies in Women's Literature* 3.1–2 (1984): 79–97.

Marshall, Paule. *Brown Girl, Brownstones*. 1959. Old Westbury, NY: Feminist Press, 1981.

———. *The Chosen Place, the Timeless People*. New York: Harcourt, 1969.

———. "From the Poets in the Kitchen." *Reena* 3–24.

———. Personal interview. 17 March 1988.

———. *Praisesong for the Widow*. New York: Putnam's, 1983.

———. *Reena*. Old Westbury, NY: Feminist Press, 1983.

———. "Shaping the World of My Art." *New Letters* 40.1 (1973): 97–112.

———. "To Da-duh, in Memorium." Reena 95–106.

McAdoo, Harriette, ed. *Black Families*. Beverly Hills: Sage Publications, 1981.

Mere, Ada. "The Unique Role of Women in Nation Building." Unpublished paper. U of Nigeria, 1984.

Morrison, Toni. *Beloved*. New York: Knopf, 1987.

———. "Rootedness: The Ancestor as Foundation." Evans 339–45.

———. *Song of Solomon*. New York: New American Library, 1977.

———. *Sula*. New York: Bantam Books, 1973.

———. *Tar Baby*. New York: New American Library, 1981.

Moynihan, Daniel. *The Negro Family: A Case for National Action*. U.S. Dept. of Labor. Office of Policy, Planning, and Research. March 1965.

Mphahlele, Ezekiel. *The African Image*. London: Faber and Faber, 1962.

Nagenda, John. "Generations in Conflict." *Protest and Conflict in African Literature*. Ed. Donald Munro and Cosmos Pieterse. New York: Africana Publishing, 1969. 101–108.

Nandakumar, Prema. "An Image of African Womanhood: A Study of Flora Nwapa's *Efuru*." *African Quarterly* 11 (1971): 136–46.

Nichols, Lee. *African Writers at the Microphone*. Washington, DC: Three Continents Press, 1984.

———. *Conversations with African Writers*. Washington, DC: Voice of America, 1981.

Nwapa, Flora. *Efuru*. London: Heinemann, 1966.

———. *Idu*. London: Heinemann, 1970.

———. *Mammy Water*. Enugu, Nigeria: Tana Press, 1979.

———. Personal interviews. March–July 1984.

———. *Wives at War*. Enugu, Nigeria: Tana Press, 1981.

Nwoga, Donatus. "The Chi, Individualism and Igbo Religion: A Comment." *Conch* 3.2 (1971): 118–20.

———. Personal interviews. Nov. 1983–June 1984.

Obiechina, Emmanuel. *Culture, Tradition and Society in the West African Novel*. London: Cambridge UP, 1975.

O'Brien, John, ed. *Interviews with Black Writers*. New York: Liveright, 1973.

Okonjo, Kamene. "Aspects of Continuity and Change in Mate Selection among the Igbo West of the River Niger." Unpublished paper. U of Nigeria, 1978.

———. "The Place of Decision-making in the Rural Igbo Family." Unpublished paper. U of Nigeria, 1984.

———. "Sex Roles in Nigerian Politics." Oppong 212–21.

Okonkwo, Juliet. "Adam and Eve: Igbo Marriage in the Nigerian Novel." *Conch* 3.2 (1971): 137–51.

———. "The Talented Woman in African Literature." *Africa Quarterly* 15.4 (1976): 36–47.

Okyea, E. Ofori. "The Atwia-Ekumfi Kodzidan—An Experimental African Theatre." *Okyeame* 4.1 (1970): 82–85.

Ong, Walter J. *Orality and Literacy*. London: Methuen, 1982.

Oppong, Christine, ed. *Female and Male in West Africa*. London: George Allen, 1983.

O'Shaughnessy, Kathleen. "'Life, life, life, life': The Community as Chorus in *Song of Solomon*." *Critical Essays on Toni Morrison*. Ed. Nellie Y. McKay. Boston: G. K. Hall, 1988. 125–33.

Palmer, Eustace. Rev. of Elechi Amadi, *The Concubine* and Flora Nwapa, *Efuru*. *African Literature Today* 1 (1968): 56–58.

Pettis, Joyce. "The Ancestor in Paule Marshall's *Praisesong for the Widow*." Conference on Black Writers and Their Sources, North Carolina Central U. 25 Sept. 1985.

Pollard, Velma. "Cultural Connections in Paula Marshall's *Praisesong for the Widow*." *World Literature Written in English* 25.2 (1985): 285–98.

Price, Reynolds. Rev. of *Song of Solomon*. *New York Times Book Review* 11 Sept. 1977: 48–50.

Pryse, Marjorie, and Hortense J. Spillers, eds. *Conjuring: Black Women, Fiction, and Literary Tradition*. Bloomington: Indiana UP, 1985.

Ray, Benjamin. *African Religions: Symbol, Ritual and Community*. Englewood Cliffs, NJ: Prentice, 1976.

Reagon, Bernice Johnson. "African Diaspora Women: The Making of Cultural Workers." *Women in Africa and the Diaspora*. Ed. Rosalyn Terborg-Penn, Sharon Harley, and Andrea Benton Rushing. Washington: Howard UP, 1987. 167–80.

———. "My Black Mothers and Sisters: On Beginning a Cultural Autobiography." *Feminist Studies* 8 (Spring 1982): 81–96.

Robinson, Lillian. *Sex, Class and Culture*. Bloomington: Indiana UP, 1978.

Rodgers-Rose, La Frances. *The Black Woman*. Beverly Hills: Sage Publications, 1980.

Rushing, Andrea Benton. "Family Resemblances: A Comparative Study of Women Protagonists in Contemporary African American and Anglophone African Novels." Diss. U of Massachusetts, 1983.

Sandiford, Keith A. "Paule Marshall's *Praisesong for the Widow*: The Reluctant Heiress, or Whose Life Is It Anyway?" *Black American Literature Forum* 20.4 (1986): 371–92.

Scheub, Harold. "Two African Women." *Revue des Langues Vivantes* 37.5 (1971): 545–58.

Schipper, Mineke, ed. *Unheard Words: Women and Literature in Africa, the Arab World, Asia, the Caribbean and Latin America*. Trans. Barbara Potter Fasting. London: Allison and Busby, 1985.

Schmidt, Nancy. "African Women Writers of Literature for Children." *World Literature Written in English* 17.1 (1978): 7–21.

Skerrett, Joseph T. "Recitations to the *Griot*: Storytelling and Learning in Toni Morrison's *Song of Solomon*." Pryse 192–202.

Smith, Barbara. "Towards a Black Feminist Criticism." Hull 157–75.

Sofọla, 'Zulu. Personal Interviews. 23 Feb. and 16 June 1984.

Sọyinka, Wole. *Myth, Literature and the African World View*. London: Cambridge UP, 1976.

Steady, Filomina Chioma, ed. *The Black Woman Cross-Culturally*. Boston: Schenkman, 1981.

Stepto, Robert. "Intimate Things in Place." *Massachusetts Review* 18 (1977): 473–89.

Strouse, Jean. "Toni Morrison's Black Magic." *Newsweek* 30 March 1981: 50–53.

Sudarkasa, Niara. "Female Employment and Family Organization in West Africa." Steady 49–64.

———. "Interpreting the African Heritage in Afro-American Family Organization." McAdoo 38–50.

Sutherland, Efua. *Edufa*. London: Longman, 1967.

———. *Foriwa*. Accra: Ghana Publishing, 1967.

———. Interview. With Maxine Lautré. Duerden 183–85.

———. *The Marriage of Anansewa*. Washington, DC: Three Continents Press, 1975.

———. "New Life in Kyerefaso." *An African Treasury*. Ed. Langston Hughes. New York: Brown Publishing, 1960. 11–117.

Taiwo, Oladele. *Female Writers of Modern Africa*. London: Macmillan, 1984.

Tanner, Nancy. "Matrifocality in Indonesia and Africa and among Black Americans." *Women, Culture and Society*. Ed. Michele Rosaldo and Louise Lamphere. Stanford, CA: Stanford UP, 1974. 129–56.

Tate, Claudia, ed. *Black Woman Writers at Work*. New York: Continuum, 1983.

Thompson, Robert Farris. *Flash of the Spirit*. New York: Vintage Books, 1984.

Trinh T. Minh-ha. *Woman, Native, Other*. Bloomington: Indiana UP, 1989.

Tutuola, Amos. *The Palm-Wine Drinkard*. London: Faber and Faber,

1952.

Uchendu, Victor. *The Igbo of Southeast Nigeria*. New York: Holt, 1965.

Vansina, Jan. *Oral Tradition as History*. Madison: U of Wisconsin P, 1985.

Vellenga, Dorothy Dee. "Who Is a Wife? Legal Expressions of Heterosexual Conflict in Ghana." Oppong 144–55.

Vincent, Theo. *Seventeen Black and African Writers on Literature and Life*. Lagos: Cross Continent Press, 1981.

Wades-Gayles, Gloria. *No Crystal Stair: Visions of Race and Sex in Black Women's Fiction*. New York: Pilgrim's Press, 1984.

Walker, Alice. *The Color Purple*. New York: Harcourt, 1982.

———. *In Love and Trouble*. New York: Harcourt, 1973.

———. *In Search of Our Mothers' Gardens*. New York: Harcourt, 1983.

———. Interview. With Peter Prescott. *Newsweek* 21 July 1982: 67.

———. *Meridian*. New York: Harcourt, 1976.

———. *The Temple of My Familiar*. New York: Harcourt, 1989.

———. *The Third Life of Grange Copeland*. New York: Harcourt, 1970.

Wall, Cheryl, ed. *Changing Our Own Words: Essays on Criticism, Theory, and Writing by Black Women*. New Brunswick: Rutgers UP, 1989.

Washington, Mary Helen. "Afterword." *Brown Girl, Brownstones*. By Paule Marshall. 311–24.

———. "Teaching BLACK-EYED SUSANS: An Approach to the Study of Black Woman Writers." Hull 208–20.

Watkins, Mel. "Talk with Toni Morrison." *New York Times Book Review* 11 Sept. 1977: 48; 50.

Wideman, John Edgar. *Damballah*. New York: Avon, 1981.

———. *Homewood Trilogy*. New York: Avon, 1984.

Williams, Raymond. *Marxism and Literature*. New York: Oxford UP, 1977.

———. *Problems in Materialism and Culture*. London: NLB, 1980.

Woolf, Virginia. *A Room of One's Own*. New York: Harcourt, 1929.

Young, Virginia Heyer. "Family and Childhood in a Southern Negro Community." *American Anthropology* 72 (1970): 269–87.

# INDEX